The Legend of Death

The Legend of Death

Two Poetic Sequences

JOHN MILBANK

CASCADE *Books* • Eugene, Oregon

THE LEGEND OF DEATH
Two Poetic Sequences

Copyright © 2008 John Milbank. All rights reserved. Except for brief quotations in critical publications or reviews, no part of this book may be reproduced in any manner without prior written permission from the publisher. Write: Permissions, Wipf and Stock Publishers, 199 W. 8th Ave., Suite 3, Eugene, OR 97401.

Cascade Books
A Division of Wipf and Stock Publishers
199 W. 8th Ave., Suite 3
Eugene, OR 97401

www.wipfandstock.com

ISBN 13: 978-1-55635-915-6

Cataloging-in-Publication data:

Milbank, John.

    The legend of death : two poetic sequences / John Milbank.

    x + 182 p. ; 23 cm. —

    ISBN 13: 978-1-55635-915-6

    1. Poetry—21st century—Collections. I. Title.

PR6063. I29 L41 2008

Manufactured in the U.S.A.

In Memory of Polly

Contents

On the Diagonal ∼ Metaphysical Landscapes

Preface ∼ *The Eight Diagonals*   2

    The Diary of the Birds   8
    Early Autumn Vagrant   10
    Dwelling   11
    Exchange   12
    Southwards   13
    At Castlefreke   14
    Fen-sky above Cambridge   18
    Beribboned   19
    South of Newmarket   20
    Transport   22
    North Riding   23
    The Dream of the Wolds   24
    Three Revelations in Gloucestershire   26
    Inner Hebrides   27
    Ode to Night   28
    Global Warming   29
    The Splendid Quest   31
    Immanent Consistencies   33
    Return to Zion   34
    Winter Interior   35
    Poe Contemplates the Republic in Albemarle County   36
    The Appalachian Forest   37
    A Michaelmas Round   38

The Market Cart (On the Painting by Thomas Gainsborough)   40
The Consolation of North Norfolk   42
East Mercia   44
The Dean's Twilight   46
Turnings   49
Virginian Eschatology   53
The Inn of the World in the Wolds of Lincolnshire   54
The Shire's Ages (Between Trent and Sherwood)   57
Hymn to Iamblichus on May Morning   60
Ode: the Poem of the Path   62
On the Diagonal   68
On the Lizard   70
The Shire Wood   71
Ode to Sorrow   74
North of the Trent   75
Participation in the Périgord   77
Cosmos   82
Threddlethorpe Sands   83
Rogationtide in England   86
Numbered   88
The Perfect Evening   89
Downland Twilight   90
The Winter Dyke   91
Still March Maiden   92
Ode to Flanders   93
Exile   95
Sintra   98
Fenland Inventory   99
London Baroque   100
Awake   101
The English Cadence   102
Deliverance   103
The Fiery Mountain   104
A Visit to Winter   105

The Night-Bee   107

Moongarm   108

The Houses of Virginia   110

The Dream of Emerald   111

Via Moderna   113

Beware of the Snakes   114

South Cotswolds: Early Springtime   116

Biology   117

Ode to Celandines   118

Local Apocalypse   119

The Earthly Paradise   120

The Doom of Mortals   122

Around Sidmouth   124

One Green Day   126

The Legend of Death

Preface ~ The Vessel and the Ring   128

    1. The Legend of Death   134

    2. The Rumour of Life   142

    3. The Birth of Romance   149

    4. The Quest of the Vessel   154

    5. The Advent Train-Ride   160

    6. The Song of Weyland   168

    7. The Circulation of the Ring   172

    8. In the Land of the East Angles   176

    9. The Butterflies at Dyke's End   179

    Notes on Places and Sources   182

On the Diagonal
Metaphysical Landscapes

Preface

THE EIGHT DIAGONALS

The eight poetic diagonals are culture, the preternatural, religion, synaesthesia, onomatopoeia, the imagination, spatio-temporal synthesis, and justice.

1. Human beings, as they now know all too well, live on the frail surface of the earth; amongst animal species they are one of the physically most vulnerable. Yet this thin crust of organic matter and the still thinner crust of the spirit is the most concentrated, the most sensitive, and the most suggestive part of the cosmos. It in every way exceeds itself in pointing above its horizontal surface towards vertical transcendence. However, it can never leave itself behind and always carries itself with itself in every ascent. Poetry attends to the resultant human diagonal. It has to do with the eternal, with the concentrations of ideas, with the multiple and specific abstractions ignored by science. But it also has to do with memory, with anecdote, and with invocation of sensory presence.

2. This poetic diagonal is humanity, and therefore it is also culture. Yet the diagonal ascent of culture is always properly thwarted by its horizontal base, else it would be but vertical and irreversible lift-off. A diagonal in order to be a diagonal is fractalized, such that, in the present case, another diagonal opens up between culture and nature. This diagonal too belongs to poetry, but it tends to pull poetry away from the sphere of the supernatural (and the publicly religious) back towards that which in nature seems to be as yet unfathomed, to a preternatural sense of an otherness lurking behind natural appearances. Cultural processes may draw out the meanings latent in nature, but poetry retains the sense that there is an excess of meaning and of hidden intelligent life within the natural world that culture can never fully fathom. This pays tribute to the inexhaustibility, diversity and mystery of the divine creation. At the same time, human beings properly consider that their work is to complete nature, to bring it to its aesthetic consummation. In addition, they are called upon to repair nature, which shares in the general but contingent fallenness of the created order. In all these ways poetry describes

a diagonal between nature and culture that may be expressed in the metaphoric figures of "twilight" and "horizon"—an impossible "between" that yet leaks out to us certain secreted meanings. Through a constant transference of tropes between the natural and the cultural, the former is seen as the divine artefact that we must perfect, while the latter is seen as the elusiveness of human "nature," which we struggle to find and to express. In searching endlessly for our "right places" in space and our "right measures" in time, we search also to glorify and rectify the entire cosmos. Herein lies the most authentic and not merely subjective meaning of the "psychogeographical."

3. Besides our sense of a hidden excessive meaning within nature, we have equally a sense of a deficiency of meaning there—of a flatness, a banality of sheer factuality that can intrude upon the brightest day (or perhaps more upon a bright day than a shadowed one). Theology understands this in terms of the fallenness of things. Yet there is equally a fallenness of signs: for if facts seem deficient in significance, then equally signs seem deficient in reality. An unbridgeable "parallax" seems to open up here, and human beings characteristically divide their time between the real that cannot be ignored but does not seem to matter, and fictions that are consoling and richly meaningful and yet untrue, or as yet unrealized. Here, however, poetry seeks to trace the third diagonal: the middle path of dream between the real and the fictional that would expose both as but partial aspects of a higher and suppressed "super-real." And the latter is indeed both the elusive goal and the obscure assumption of all religion: a finally meaningful real, a mattering that is, indeed, also matter, also the real ground beneath our feet. In consequence, the writing of poetry hovers between the invocation of real phenomenal presences on the one hand, and narrations that mingle the historical with the fantastic, and the actual with the possible, on the other. Yet it is most itself when it returns from both the lyrically descriptive and the epically diegetic (or the dramatically performative) to the apostrophic address to created things, or the hymnic address to created and uncreated spirits. This supplies the supreme poetic idiom that is the "ode": at once invocatory address and "path" for the addressor and (sometimes) the addressee. Here description and fiction are both fulfilled and surpassed in the praise of the super-real, which is also fully meaningful. And for finite human beings it is the ode that calls the object of the ode into presence for us.

4. How is this voice of calling realized? In this case one must recognize that the diagonal of ascent is not simply a vertical, precisely because it is com-

posed of all the seemingly meagre provisions of the horizontal: of the fragile, tenuous green surface of the earth. Poetry is not the art of the mind, a painting in spiritual meanings; on the contrary, it is the bastard art of the fourth diagonal, which is that traced across all of our five senses. There are legitimate arts of vision, of hearing, of tasting, of touching, and of smelling. But poetry must perforce pretend through virtual imitation to possess the skills of the painter, the composer, the chef, the lover, and the distiller of perfumes. More especially, the poet composes a kind of restricted music whose notes, punctuated bars and syncopations are somehow invoked visual images (primarily), besides sensations of touch, taste, and odour. But by weaving across the sensory boundaries where there is in fact no sensory space available, this "common sensing," as Plato and Aristotle taught, actually "proves" the soul, declares the reality of mind and spirit. So if the proper yet bastard sphere of poetry is *sensus communis*, then poetry is the original operation of human thinking as such, its original illegitimacy that is yet the highest created birthright.

5. For this reason, synaesthesia also shows "Cratylism"—or the belief that there is a more than arbitrary link between the sound of words and the nature of things—to be no illusion. For if language is not "onomatopoeic" in this extended sense (beyond the mere echo in words of natural sounds) there could be no human thought at all, vindicating the insights of Stephan Mallarmé and Arthur Rimbaud. This is because it is the event of speech alone that at once proves and realizes the occurrence of "common sensing." But of course this onomatopoeic effect cannot be consistently proved, even if many consistent patterns in language suggest it. This is precisely because we have no sheerly non-linguistic access to things and the ideas of things, and therefore cannot fully compare things to words, since the latter have already biased our sense of the real. This biasing is multiply inflected by the variety of the many different human languages, even though this variety does not disprove the "Cratylist" perspective, but rather tends to indicate the different aspects of the essences of things that different tongues reveal—as Mallarmé the Frenchman noted in his exploration, in *Les Mots Anglais*, of the consistent onomatopoeic families into which English words tend to fall. Poetry, however, is the closest possible approach to the proof of Cratylism—for it at once uncovers, intensifies, and reaffirms the onomatopoeic effect. This is not truly a mirroring "representation" of things by words (as if we could ever really fully compare the one with the other), but rather a necessary "diagonal" blending of things and words that simultaneously declares and elevates them both.

6. Poetry, therefore, first invented language as the onomatopoeic expression of our common sensing. This is why, for Shelley, evoking the myth of Orpheus, whose music charmed the walls of cities into being, poets are "the unacknowledged legislators of the world." (This had nothing to do with romantic hubris, as is so often supposed.) But by inventing language, poetry intimated our participation in the realm of spirit, our possession of rational souls. Once this had occurred, a sixth diagonal relationship opened up between the mind on the one hand, and matter and sensing on the other. Here again, it would seem that there can be no mediation, and yet poetry is the impossible possibility and necessity of just such a mediation. Through its tropes, poetry constantly objectifies the spiritual in order that it can exist on earth at all, while it equally spiritualizes the material in order that its meaning may be realized. This can be neither the work of sensing nor of pure thought: rather, it is the work of a common sensing, which is always already doubled by the work of the imagination. For if it is possible for the senses to sense all together—for the sight therefore in some sense to hear, the ears to see, and so forth, as Baudelaire realized (such that we all in reality suffer from this pathology, albeit that only a few are consciously "afflicted" by it, to their artistic advantage, like the composer Messiaen)—then this must occur invisibly, inaudibly and so forth. But if common sensing can occur in this way, then it also always shadows the senses, accompanies every sensation with a commonly-inflected sensation that can also be repeated in the absence of the sensed object. Here we have, in the first case, Aquinas's "return to the phantasm" that completes every act of understanding, which is also Coleridge's "primary imagination." In the second case, we have medieval artistic "fantasy"' and Coleridge's "secondary imagination." But in either case we are talking about the ability of the mind itself to see, to hear, to taste, to feel, and to smell, and all of these only because it is able to combine them. Thus, for example, the mind cannot envisage the sea without also smelling the brine, hearing the waves roar, feeling both its threat and promise to the touch. In such mental images we have the twilight threshold between sensing and thinking, the horizon between matter and spirit itself. It is for this reason that the imagination is strangely both passive and active, within our control and outside it: both something that occurs to us and something we can shape—a wholly dream-like reality that yet shadows all our everyday and alone renders it possible at all. Images are the beginning of ideas, just as poetry distills from the world its universal colours, misty effluents, and complex geometric shapes. However, because humanity exists on a diagonal,

it must always return from ideas to imaginings if it is to have any vehicle for assent to that supreme origin that is the source of the material as well as the spiritual. This can be poetically extended still further by a *chiasmus* between the sensing human creature and the world that is sensed: our return to the image leads us back beyond it to the sensed objects, such that it is as if they are sensing us, rather than us sensing them. Here we realize that our diagonal is also a fold in the fragile surface of the earth.

7. If poetry is caught primarily between music and painting, then it is also caught between time and space. There lies the sixth diagonal that it must trace as an "impossible" mediation. Only through this mediation can it in fact achieve the primary diagonal, which is the cultural ascent from finitude to the transcendent infinite. For to attain this, we must not sustain the illusion of a stable present: humans, as all of them poets, must "let time pass," express reality as musical flow if they are to see that it is but a fleeting image of the eternal, as Plato taught. On the other hand, were we to conceive of poetry only as music, with a sheerly ineffable meaning (and in this sense even music is not entirely music), then we would fall prey to a cult of the pure flow, whose movement would triumph in empty significance over anything that it flowed through or flowed over. Time as movement can only point to the infinitely abiding (and yet most fully energetic) because this movement is but the link of all its way-stations, whose numbers infinitely fractalize, and yet are not entirely illusory, precisely because they also image eternity. The passing flow images eternity in its boundlessness and inexhaustibility, whereas the temporary presences—which stay and yet sustain temporal movement—image eternity's *nunc stans*, as Boethius expressed it. Poetry must therefore celebrate them also, yet no single one or group of them exclusively, for fear of idolatry. And to stay for a moment in time is to turn off the track of time into the temporary shelter of space. In verbal poetry it is to interrupt the flow of rhythm (and yet to constitute it through punctuation) by evoking the visual image—or the olfactory or tactile sensation. The flow of time is also experienced by human beings as the inward flow of emotional experience. But once more, this would lose shape and coherence, or any indication beyond itself, were it not for formal expression in words that take shape within space and which invoke concrete spatial realities. Poetry searches that point where spontaneity and form are one: where the form that is chosen and emerges is the form that reveals an experience or a feeling more clearly; the form that tempers or consoles emotion and yet also for the first time fully realizes it.

8. Finally, the aesthetic sense of finding the right placement precisely overlaps with the human ethical sense. Accordingly, the eighth poetic diagonal—lying eschatologically beyond the poetic—is justice. For Aristotle in the Nicomachean Ethics, distributive justice concerns the analogy that exists between quantitatively different distributions of position or reward to different individuals or groups, according to their capacities and desert. Although the things distributed differ, there can be an analogical proportion between the ratios that pertain between persons and what have been apportioned to them. The portion accorded to a doctor may differ from that accorded to a seaman (though this difference may not necessarily be one of inequality) and yet there may be an equity between the two apportionings in so far as a principle of "appropriateness" has been applied in either case. For Aristotle, this non-quantifiable comparison (for he is not speaking of exactly equivalent ratios) is a "diagonal." Hence for him justice did not consist in people being accorded their places within a square bounded by horizontal and vertical lines that might provide a grid for exact, measurable placings. Rather, it was the diagonal that can escape the square that brought about the original distribution, according to no exactly circumscribed rule. If one links this with the modern mathematical idea of the way a sub-set can "diagonalize out" of a containing set, such that the contained may paradoxically exceed the container, then we can say that the ethical "rule of the diagonal" ensures that it is the exception that will always "prove the rule." For the Aristotelian sense of equity, being a Lesbian rule, is only confirmed, again and again, by the very instance of its application. Similarly, the poetic traversing of the first seven diagonals obeys no prescribed law, but must ceaselessly make the law, precisely by always exceeding any harmony or mode of regularity so far known about. It represents the true order beyond order and its rule is at one with outlawry. Yet this is not to affirm an *aporia* that licenses anarchy, any more than spontaneity and form are in any necessary ultimate tension. Rather, every new exceptional instance of order, in order to be order at all, must exhibit some coherence with the unique orders already established. Every real new poem is only such by the way in which it further composes the one long continuous poem which is human culture itself, the first diagonal. And it is because poetry is the first language that it is also, as I have already said, the first law. Hence a true aesthetic distribution constrains us inwardly, and so gives rise to an ethical imperative, which also desires that there should arise further works that strive for perfection. These true works are works that human beings might adequately inhabit: the carapaces of human justice.

THE DIARY OF THE BIRDS

The new leaves laid out
in bound series
of a blanched Spring before the Spring
that is preparing beneath
its ranked, ranged frost and snow-strata.

One page a day:
this may retard
my linear hurtle towards death
by a stately passage
through the ecclesiastical cycles.

The weeks forgotten, obscured
in a spacious arrangement of serious
small roundings of light and darkness.
One spread a week will not this year
paste-out my would-be densities.

But on every page henceforth
there will appear a deed,
a weighted sentiment;
at nightfall a lapse to peace
after genuine ponder,
like my old dream to dwell within
the British Birds' pictures:
their several mists,
unique arrangements of twigs' partings,
surrounded by scarlet berries, or else the
threadbare dangling seeds

of the earliest Springtime.
Which to be in?
An agony of hesitation
squandered since I could never be privileged
to render such election,

exactly as I wonder now
which bleak perfect day to commence with already,
under cover of which pure fog's rank
absolutely serried by position
and previous divine-human sortilege.

Not that I would be a bird;
rather retain a totemic option on nesting
and re-construe flight as the distance
and privilege of uninvested spirit
that constitutes our *humanum*.

Nor would I have these leaves already budded,
lost to risky investments in pleasure of recall
that is but anticipated melancholia.
Yet I would like already to settle
upon their emerging greens—

lincoln, olive, emerald,
in their freshness of surprise
that might enchant and enrapture
without dire wakefulness
my pure white hibernation.

EARLY AUTUMN VAGRANT

A day brushed with lemon.

Luminous wafts
of light lapping frequently
like inverted shadows
beneath a dull-cast heaven.

All ignored by the brimming
schemes of afternoon pastures

for their harvest of sun-tide,
with wave after wave of
wind at last blindly illuming

the bench of the end of everything:
all cast-up, awaiting unknown salvage.

It has all been perfect,
but has left me languished,

my world swept away from me
and myself along with it.
My bodily eyes, self-bereft,
watch my soul depart on its last
and surest voyaging,

while I read on eagerly
in the book about love
as the dusk sweeps out
the open clearness.

DWELLING

Black wings luring the landscape,
now glimpsed through the windows
of a passing train-carriage,
borne along for a while
like a detached segment of England,
then released back to the previous moment
of whence and whither.

Locked in the shining casket of the one place,
yet gloriously forth from it.
So the breeze has arisen from the earth
in a sudden gust of upward seizure,
invading the heavenly with its clear smoke,
just as this poem belongs here in the house with me,
and its words fit the faint-painted walls.

I cannot tell why they have always been here,
but I am glad about it.
I saw them here eternally from across the river
in the bright place—they were there:
the miracle of life's always breaking horizon
above the horrible depths
and beneath the passionless sky.

EXCHANGE

Our words can be but sacrifice
to one unknown,

as the land goes on being the same
right to the end of the peninsula:
the even grass, the same sheep cropping;
then the cliff's edge plunge to the waters
that is unannounced in the earth's language.

And yet the sea delivers the earth
by a gradual landing
that is magical metamorphosis:

first in the fine wet sand,
scarcely treadable,
like a material our toes are dreaming
for their prone consolation.

And later by the hidden path up the cliff's face
she has herself long scoured,
and later still in the lingering penetrations of sea-fret
through all our dreams, out of which
a lighter not yet fully-inward dawn
is the next day imperceptibly distilled.

In this way alone our words can cease to be
pure gamble and entreaty,
when their plea awakens from drowning
to discover that this loss is the manifold gradual way
of divine speech rendering our very own
porous solidity.

SOUTHWARDS

Weep daughter perhaps,
for the man with the iced bun has his eye upon you,

slung across the back of his Porsche,
oblivious to the roar of the lorries
on the Great North Road
where it has lost being a motorway for a while
but will be again, in a new lucid interval
without respite of halts for ancient livery
startlingly and enchantingly too near the traffic,
nor spawning lay-bys like drained ox-bows.

He is thinking that therein lies his chance.
That there is always the future.

AT CASTLEFREKE

It is never good to change a basic pattern;
your only chance lies with more variations.
Later, the whole will constitute something different,
unimagined until others hear it,
entirely to their surprised likings.

Like the long strand and the aching dunes,
creeks winding to inland emerald seas of vistas.
The salt-dried forests of brittle fir-trees,
the welcome clumps of beech and the displaced bamboo track
to the ruined churches.

Yet not the old castle neglected for the new house
now itself abandoned to shelter the orange villa
within its decayed gums
like a succulent sweet whose resented temptation
can never be bitten into.

While the dunes and the woods seem a temporary boundary
that cannot quite construe
the puzzling arrangement of waters.

What matters is the green sea that later resumes
as the blue mountains,
their waves always restrained in the distance,
always circling around the lush bog-land.
Here the curious lilts of road and pasture
are forever dreaming of a way to sustain their humility,
thereby dominating the high hills,
rendering them temporary, like the sea's rising.

For not the heights triumph here,
though neither are they denied.
Finally they ornament a broad yielding
and a surging sideways.

The houses of the townships
position themselves before each other,
connected in the web of their mutual
keeping of a generous distance.

Sometimes, in centuries,
this has turned sinister.

And when the absentee and brutal
came to outnumber the improving landlords,
improvement was gradually abandoned
for the purchase of purity.

So no pathways are any longer maintained here.
The copses decay and
expensive bungalows break the skein
of mutual observances.

Alba laments what she did not do for Erin
and what she did indeed do to her,
while Erin still flows into Alba enriching her.
But for all this one registers the sadness
of an unnatural divorce
and a want in Erin of what
Alba must still mean to her,

since these two have been bound together
and loosed from each other
a thousand times since the druids
studied in Alba but ruled here in Erin.

Now in Alba there is a pride in rule without learning,
and in Erin a pride in rhetoric without governance;
a gash in the one rock: a cruel exposure.
Sea and sky close over the lone pupil,
and the iris runs endlessly into the dark cave.
Wave after wave succeeds, like hands caressing;
always the next stroke a little too late
and so all the more wanted.
And the distances between the waves
to the eye still perfect because of this.

Glimpsed from the headland's height
in the windy night, the lightened wind,
the rush of light, the breeze gleaming
above the bay's pure circle
which enters like reason
upon the confusions of landscape,

an inner movement surging to its prow,
sublated always in the circular goal and origin.

Yet the rocks offer their jagged widened lips
with a thousand alarms that are
inseparable from a thousand shelterings
for the risked entrance and fusion.

What raises the tower
causes also the sea to swell around it.
Entry is by wild restraint
here and since the reincarnate always.

FEN-SKY ABOVE CAMBRIDGE

Maybe
      the clouds are rising
  treetops
         whose levitation
hovers like
      the almost landing

of a heavenly vision
so close
    so
        mockingly distant,

forever watching
        so much
            since aeons
that we have forgotten
to discern their angel eyes
          here.

BERIBBONED

Liquid drenched gloss
over the shrubbery
defies and vindicates
a grey dawning.

She has caught
Nature's purposes
by securing a hollyhock
to the clothesline.

So which is the stalk
and which the measure?
Even her clothes-pegs
are not neglected

but attended precisely
by plump wooden ladybirds.
Pear trees grow
beribboned, naturally.

SOUTH OF NEWMARKET

To seek the place of escape:
fields lifted, expectant like words
on their own golden plains,
oddly separated from each other
as if each one announced again 'field'
and inserted this idea
awkwardly into the landscape,
assisted and hindered equally
by dark-green hedges and bristling
multi-emptied copses.

Here no hills nor plains
reveal the distant perspective.
And so every village appears
precarious, too-little raised
above the earth
which forever reclaims it,
and tall trees but miniatures
of what they are
supposed to be and may become
in memory or painting.

Therefore no imagining arises
of the next settlement; this is the all of England.
The ordered agriculture seems snatched
for the occupation of a single moment
and a brief tract of sliding greens and golds,
with here a remarkable tower uplifted
from encroaching husbandry
so that its cosmic urbanity is always hovering
to render the isolation and twilight an uncanny miracle
of rapt cart-track and virgin graveyard.

TRANSPORT

Metaphor cannot disappoint
as it swerves away
from the tarmac.

The tarmac cannot disappoint
in its literality.

When both eventually disappoint
(the empty charm and the charmless empty),
we consider flinging ourselves
in the path of other automobiles,

to receive a pain that would instantly
collapse forever
under the weight of its own prescience,

in despair of a literal swerving
upon the metaphoric ground, imagined.

So may these words convey nonetheless such a dream
in some found measure
to lost souls, this Adonian evening.

NORTH RIDING

Little twists of lanes
like corkscrews of light-green sherbet
secreted in the rock-sides.

Moorland tabletops cranked open
to reveal the sunken hills
nestling in strangely fertile canyons.

Green necks of fields scarving the
near horizon; fretted with stone walls
that render obscure fervour.

Red tiles since Roman times
that helmet with deserted peace composed settlements
built with small stones well-exacted.

Rural order russet and enduring in
local majesty of generous extension.
The north's sweep's pride in the return of craftwork,

in bevelled tabletops like the sure-dipping
sheep-runs. The soul readies itself to respond well
to the rupture of all reverence.

THE DREAM OF THE WOLDS

Here is forgotten about,
soft sinking of old faded hills,

now merged with mist—
a vague heart, hardly asserted.

A need of the sense of angels observing;
else we will mimic
unto shame and oblivion,

urged to accumulate
till we sift only the abstract that is
lodged in a contrived impermanence.

Yet if we let pass,
dreaming our half-death as a spectacle
for those others about us,

then we re-establish the red-brick farmstead,
warm in its dwelling and its outhouses also,

as they cluster together above the swerves of the road,
guarding the huge gentle chasm of landsweep

that inverts as a twisting slope through the tufted woodland,
to provide a reverie of church-tower, blueness above it—
with white mist encroaching.

Here opening trees throng in the
lands of East Mercia. Thinning northward
before the criss-cross fields take over,

while the glassy drive across unvisited England
refuses to accrue to my own span only.
This deep vague folding is always of another flock,

for after failure of fathers, wary of trespass,
far steps do not outrun a distant reaching

down to us heartward, the sudden plunge of the car
and the sudden sight of the towers: Melton Mowbray's
grace-casket, tripled and castling.

THREE REVELATIONS
IN GLOUCESTERSHIRE

Crimped oak-tree
by the centuries set
with slow lightning,
whose zigzags are as sure
as they are sudden.

The shock of endurance.
Pure gold pours gift
of the sun's cornlight
through the slatternly opening
of the slanting gateposts.

The bold of the evening.
Broad original shadow
extends the wood's domain
over the golden stubble
in the passing twilight.

A rare, a ravishing most secret.

INNER HEBRIDES

Dark and wild,
the wood furled
seeking
        the crystal waves'
passion
        in thickets of thorn-blooms

that sprout up from blood-flares
in the blue dusk

now shone-forth
                with tumult,
starlight's clamour
            and piercing.

All the night
he ranged ceaselessly
                      about the near islands,
and in the daylight delivered
his far spoils
        for the Kingdom.

ODE TO NIGHT

Night from dawn already
I seek your harbour

of full ocean roaring
to blend and tumble

our sound passions of daylight
lost in such rational confusions of

darkness wherein perhaps we meet
the old lost ones and harness

the wild absolute hovering

still all about us.

GLOBAL WARMING

As the flood-puddles receive
the shadows of hedgerows,
their brittleness resolved
in densest waters;

as we are now
like small hooded animals,
vainly seeking to avoid
our own dire trafficking,

so the glorious cascades
arrive like an ambiguous gift,
too much in response
to our hints and probes,
enquiring after ends,
pure tainted origins,
and a most blatant always.

Too much in response
to our toil for a yield
of new abundance for a while
to appease that first idol, scarcity.

Still Nature's grant though,
upon our mere occasions;
invited by us, but not by us shaped
in its mode of shadow, parades
of silver, passing so near to the earth
unaffected in eminences of purple fury,

above and all through the wintry-wired
density of copseland hillside Cotswold
with its twisted tales of branches and blackness
amongst the sudden monumental homesteads.

The old tribute of springs' rising
which the Romans sought here
for their sacred familiar,

this gift renewed again in terror
for her own appeasement,
balance, measure and restoration.

A gift to us still therefore
it must surely follow,
as the water's running through its own store of images,
silvered and electrified,

will sooth most surely.

THE SPLENDID QUEST

You were from the past
and that was your magic.

Like a conjuror you summonsed up
items from antiquity

into the post-war present.
The tarnished gleam of the old train-set

with its delicate solidity
and books of imperial adventures

like 'The Splendid Quest'.
Only you could cause the attic

to yield up such surprises
which else existed now no longer.

Now you have returned to your past
forever. Yet jarringly, these treasures survive you,

have treacherously sneaked past you
into the future, as if pastness were
a passport to evasion, and your childhood
had outlasted your wise aged dignity.

They are mine now and I may find in them
much that transpired without your notice.

They were never yours then after all:
far older than you were transport and empire,
older than you and yet far younger
in their fictioning and modelling

of all that is eternally lost and sought for.

IMMANENT CONSISTENCIES

Foliate water
dapples the tree-trunk's rotundity.

Leaves enlarge to the ambitions
of amoebas down
on the water's drifting.

'Stay for a while' permits
such swapped reflections:

a care of the world for its own
and exchanged instances,
glancing together at the for-always.

RETURN TO ZION

Bird-jubilance pierces the green
that is otherwise all-whelming.

Curves rise to lowering clouds
much confounded with tree-tops.

Such a swing, such a flirtation
with the celestial.

Such high clear voices
like well-tempered bells

forged in a crucible
of waters warmed and blown-upon,

falling in new triplets
quickened once and then a third time,

for there they are now, mother and child
in the garden with a last wave

at the first greeting.
Already on earth the final vision:

one dies serenely to be raptured,
but later drives onwards
through the clamorous evening.

WINTER INTERIOR

There is an effect of dark green like that of firs
inside a winter chamber. I cannot say
what it is.

Suddenly the promise, peace, terror of a forest
of the sure North amongst the lampstands,
behind the screens—before them strong,
vivid, lurking
like a tremendous assurance of the worth
of adventure within
and beyond its veritable danger.

That is what we should live with:
the dark green of winter in its undefeated growth,
the green of indoor games—rapt pleasures taking us
past trivial loss or passing glory.

POE CONTEMPLATES THE REPUBLIC IN ALBEMARLE COUNTY

The red river
bears the red leaves
past the red hollow
through the red creek
to the red canyon.

All the almost golden
pale of maples blare
their praise
of this scarlet company.

Over the red rocks
down the red gulf
flows the lucent water
like blood thinned to the very rarest
since it has run for so long here.

Riches of vermilion
all around me like
nature's very doomed kingdom
at the heart of the new republic.

THE APPALACHIAN FOREST

Pure height of green.
Green above growth's height.
Growth as high
as the summits of blue rock,
rusty-veined and blue-varied.
Green in such stresses,
offered as aureoles,
pale upon dark layer,
self-secreted in meadows
that may never see dancing.
Withdrawn for advantage.

A MICHAELMAS ROUND

So brown and inviting earth,
restored to its primacy amongst men;
in our hearts first outrunning
the celestial

as something inward
stokes the fire of the land,
of its deep surface to blaze out,
to enfold, to permit further
our free journeys timed
through domestic raptures held
by the embrace
of a room full of light motes
arrived once in earnest.

The angels bright burdens
here fulfilled in their influence.
Their spills for our gleaning
in emptied plenitude so detailed.

Stealthily sudden,
sure now and human,
advance upon Advent,

retrieve all dispersals,
gather up every conker,
note every leaf-shade,
memorially coded,

while paces are gatewards,
thoughts for a relish,
souls fire secret actions;
the world's crest will crown us.

So brown and inviting earth
restored to its primacy amongst men;
in our hearts first outrunning
the celestial

as something inward
stokes the fire of the land,
of its deep surface to blaze out,
to enfold, to permit further
our free journeys timed through
such amber entreaties,
shoals in pent measure.

THE MARKET CART
(On the Painting by Thomas Gainsborough)

What so little
of land remaining:
a new horizon,
the journey eastwards.

Joyfully embarked on:
the ribbon of freedom,
as the riven sky
by light fast cleaves us

to the near-far church tower
on the market road,
alone in the evening,
in the cart's pent dawdling.

Close by to leave
for a while the farmstead,
complexly planted,
secure and perilous.

A way to meet there:
exchange and parting,
while forever
sad sky vast over
us clinging lowly,
secured and cherished now;
open at twilight.

One blink a picture
proceeding, remaining.

The land is still there:
our close, vast prospect.

THE CONSOLATION
OF NORTH NORFOLK

The coast hung out to dry
in a white cosmos.......
........which folds its angel-wings
many times over our grief at loss
and torment of embarrassment
over how we have been
with the most loved ones,
the most long-expected
and irreplaceable.

It curdles these passions
to the bitter-sweet cream of *methexis*,
so that they share, brokenly,
in all-enveloping misty joy
that lies above and already all about us.

Now we are reminded of our own country
by the sea ever-lurking,
held at the unnatural distance of death,
extremely hard to reach
like the edge of another dimension.

By the land like a long, slow-shelving shore,
prepared for the waters from a long way off
yet conserving all its dryness
and not forgetting its obeisance
to the wind-god also.

By many lines scored for passages
or supports: they are here indistinguishable.
One at last wants to dwell
in the vastness of an uncertainly dominant element,
where to be near the sea already
seems to mean lying beneath it
and yet to remain within the air and
still yet huddled-fast to the meagre earth-moorings.

Never lacking for the lights of guidance:
flinty round towers like celestial lighthouses;
high clumps of woodland that ride with the wind
and roar out to sea secretly at nightfall;
the rather cradled lamps of mills and staithes,
echoed in low waters' antidotes
to the crusted-shell houses—work of seal builders
to the designs of mermen.

EAST MERCIA

The entry to Dovedale
in the island's heart.

The last secret found
at the black and silver core.

Cascade of flambeaux,
old farms and foundries

does not consume itself;
fires forward through rapture

in a long fuse of measure,
disclosing these ironlands,

the green misty sweeps
to an upswept forged tumult

of granite enforcements,
strange Mercian stonework—

Byzantine to Pagan. In
the winter light showing

the island's dark self
to itself at last shimmering,

for the first time the ancient,
steep-down from the outcrop

to the coal-fire and the enriched pheasant
devoured like a triumph

not mine, come upon me
undeserved with my own finality,

a settlement never known
at last here returned to.

THE DEAN'S TWILIGHT

It is late in the evening
but never yet night.

Sipping sherry,
riding his bicycle with a wisdom
beyond his years,

the Dean turns evasion complex,
renders compromise into metaphysics,

for this is the *via media*'s shaded hour,
when she at last speaks secret words
in the gloaming to initiates

with ironic nods, previously withheld,
to Catholic and promiscuous France,
harvesting its folk-ways
and recondite urbanity,

but reining them back
for the English palette

with such succulent sentences,
well-chewed at the back of the throat
like lozenges of perspicacity
astringently flavoured.

We shall pass forever into the twilight
and never quite disappear,
our meditation intact,
hoping still to congregate

albeit in lesser numbers
but always still more select.

As it loses most adherents,
the message is distilled
to a purer refinement,

the perfect brew
sipped in the last unspoilt
backstreet alehouse

after returning with the loyal sons
from the fourth-division fixture.

'We come together in order to agree;
we do not begin with an agreement'
he announces on the once Home Service.

(Where once a Spaniard thundered
that continuous conversation
was the refusal of the responsibility
to take the necessarily lone decision.)

Still now in the late evening
it remains as profoundly half-true
as it was back at half-time
in the drizzling afternoon.

For what shall one say
of a first agreement in love
come apart when love
seems no longer so clear
and will no longer combine us?

Perhaps there are no half-measures
doled-out from the final hostelry.
Perhaps we have forgotten
the old dancing England
of Celtic rhythms,
Romany swirls
and Iberian cadences.

TURNINGS

The skin of the shadow
in the day of dusk.

The shadow of the skin
in the dusk of dawn.

The brown earth, deeper than black,
casts its furrows for multiple pathways.

The ridges of the ploughlands
chart their own infinite earth-ocean.

Waves seeth forever on dry land
as a snapshot of turbulence:

brown waves, sumptuously churned
like the butter of rocks' secret oozings.

Measure upon measure here.......
..........of staves' crossfire in meeting musics.

Far-off the bells link underground
to their fine-cast graceful girdles.

Like the delicately raised spired-towers,
they are an after-thought of nature

for the adornment of her mere surface
so mildly and rudely turned-over

in the blink of a grey eye
between darkness and darkness.

All that the depths can offer,
their canyons of trapped radiance,

is the brief momentary escape
of a dawn's skip into a low flight-path,

yet there seems so much terrible, infinite redundancy
of unnecessary details—comets and formulae

past perpetual high chasms—for
this pale stubble to constitute the real brilliance,

a faint milky appearing,
its pure scum delectable,

little more than the water-mint
bent low beneath the watered hedgerow.

For tomorrow quite early,
we will all be departing,

after such a fuss and flutter
over temporary turbulence,

churning the brown earth
in ever more complicated patterns,

with a new mechanical rigour
forcing fields into richer ruptures

near vast piles of car-tyres close by the old cow-byre;
they have become as rustic as anything,

since they belong also to our scrapings
and scratchings upon a traceable surface.

We can rip this skin asunder,
tear our own soul's hymen

to disclose the solid only as the
inner core of destruction,

or rest content here with shadows
to enchant us like the echo of a veil.

Like the veil of an echo:
the secret dumble[1] holds in our response

where all now rises to its own surface
that was forever its concealed sinking.

At the sudden shallow pool's edge to cry silently
with the shock of shame and obscure exposure

---

1. Nottinghamshire dialect for a very deeply sunken stream such as frequently occurs in that county in the sand and clay uplands north of the river Trent.

into the developed negative
through a liquid medium, pretending the gaunt

seriousness of representation
and its own finality.

Yet the earth is turned always for lustre;
for its silver sheen, caught once by eyelight,

in token of hidden torches
scouring the deeper trench of night-line,

trail-blazing in perpetual sinews
never to be unlinked here.

Twining round, our surface
meets its other face

before it, past it, beyond it,
under, through and over it:

most fine-tuned true vapour,
which earth's dawn only intimates.

VIRGINIAN ESCHATOLOGY

It always seems to be evening—
our floating through darkness,
the clouds parted like curtains
woefully.
One takes to twilight like a child

on the road back from Williamsburg,
past places that are scarcely there
even in sheer daytime.
Lacking trysts, the traveller weaves
his own bare steps amongst
the forest-cleared conundra.

Returned to the stars nevertheless,
by which other days are conjured,
other evenings, other commencements.
The most alien sufficiency will be
there the self-same familiar glory.

A turning homewards with relief
at darkening. A drowsy *resumé*
that distils the last essentials.

THE INN OF THE WORLD IN THE WOLDS OF LINCOLNSHIRE

'But he hasn't lost his sight yet.'

'She's had the operation now.'

'Yes, on her ear.'

'Well in it, I suppose.'

In the common tongue
of languish.

Across the common terrain
by a *lingua* of asphalt,
this is all I hear
with my own sense
no doubt diminished
by imperceptible degrees
with every spiral transport.

A landscape feeding from vision

even as I glimpse it
sympathetically leaning towards twilight
already from the ashen pole
of a milky noon.

Not private this dying
across the empty white gulf.

Nor the only shared secret
of a passage of solid being
that is the same for each
yet most intimately her own.

For all nature is a winter shadow
and an exultant transfer.

Foison of empty fusion,
promise of life beyond.
The secret is not life
that's dying,
nor is this our only shared idiom.

Rather it is the wind's curve,
the given graphs of tufted woodland,
accomplishment of roads' spirals,
the trees' manes sculpted by perpetual breezes,
the fields' bends' luring
of perpetual harsh zephyrs.

Before me a gaunt inn appears on a slight rise
more marked than a mountain
against a vast sky
that hides an infinite background.

The inn of the world that is all sign,
throughout its daylight *diminuendo*,
of the evening opening
for all invisible and hidden
in a quiet that at last shall sound us

through a surrounding entrance:
lone triumph for shepherds
throughout their long watches

and glorious departure.

THE SHIRE'S AGES
(Between Trent and Sherwood)

Drift floating golds and ambers
past painted strongholds
of green and glass.

The river sidles
like an arched eyebrow fallen
to decorate
our flat passages.

Its audacious curve
unexpected, celebrated by bridges,
fringed-firm by red brick,
slithered through by barges.

Dreamt of in secret
by a sample of fishermen.

Like the unknown Minster
in its shallow wong,[2]
with its regular cascades of stone rainbows,
and its chiselled leafwork
stone-grown never to sprout-forth
save the fertile faces
unseen in mere nature.

---

2. Nottinghamshire dialect for a low-lying, secreted and concave meadow.

Dependent on lapsed Adam:
wood and gold,
grey-rock and greenwork
of such endless intrication
as defeats all *mimesis*.

Lofted towers cowering in their dell;
rumoured springs lost to all origin and re-finding.
Lonely stranded built fragments
of distant townships
sift their longings
with the forest remnants.

Cuboid and ovoid mansions
proclaim the esoteric of nature
but now athwart her.

While the low-slithering sleep
of the ancient dumbles[3]
turns Roman boundaries into treacherous rifts
awaiting new pontic combatants.

And over-dark green woodlands
rival the blushing brickwork
as though a child's sketch had restored to us
the dreamt Middle of earth
and its filled-in fertile, heroic
and sanctified ages.

---

3. See footnote to 'Turnings' above.

Awkwardly outside the law
an almost-beauty of nature mutates
into the rough charm of human custom
and charitable usage.

Till the cowslips come again to Lambley.
What is the meaning of all this?
For what do the Shire's ages
reach still?

The fine vastness.

HYMN TO IAMBLICHUS ON MAY MORNING

You who heard the carol from the high tower
and glimpsed the dance beneath it.

You who knew that the dance
is the soul's whole circuit.

But that for our embodied souls
the dance is the required medium............

spun-off in a fury,
above serene............

to allow the murmuring throng
of girls and stalwarts

from out the greenwood
with such a tremble

coursing through the dawn air
like an new era's arrival,

when beneath the higher, rarer, exaltation,
honour swerved past pride

in a wave of wonder:
people coursing like water

of the dawn's awe at itself
through their warbling voices,

past the test of death
with due prescience—

one could now go anywhere
to meet love incarnate.

Iamblichus, these new leaves were yours,
and the sumptuous blossomings

in their yet fragile blowing.
Iamblichus, O noble pagan,

pray for Magdalen tower,
pray for the future of springtime,

that the *pax Christi*
may encompass the painted girls
and the sprouting spiral.

ODE: THE POEM OF THE PATH

I

The night is never
in any instant
falling.

However much
we attend
to twilight

it will always transpire
that we have fallen asleep
before lights-out,

missed the moments
of day's death,

arrived at her bedside
too late
for her last words

only to mourn her.

However realist our mien,
we must listen instead each evening
to the dark gothic fiction

whose tale is telling
already before
we can alert our ears.

II

The path gave me
this poem.
Therefore I must
re-dedicate it
to the path.

She ran just south of Wellow,
clinging to the shallow
of a defensive rampart,

scented it seemed with
the wax of my own jacket,
although the light was obscured
by the shadows of ravens

when I abstracted her.

III

The path could not prevent me.
My steps along the path
could not avoid the night.

Nor can the swimmer sense
the tide advance.
Despite all wariness,
his body does not register
the stroke too far.

For the sea also
is a surging story,
visiting the annals with oblivion,

that alone gives days to the record,
through its ungrateful obliteration
of every washed-up nightfall.

As if robed kings
never retired to their chambers
and forced marches plundered
even the silent vigil.

IV

This poem has stolen from the path,
yet decks out its twigs
and arched shelter
with more pattern and purpose,

till a nondescript winding
becomes a line of meaning;
as I am surprised by sunset,
its orange luxury arrived already
upon the near horizon.

V

We do not watch days lengthen
from the midst of winter,
nor notice any snowdrops' crescendo.

A slow shimmer,
a gathering pulse—
we merely assume them
as we must
from their resultants.

As we miss also our lives' upshots,
since they are entirely encompassed
by another reality
which altogether owns them.

VI

This evening
the twilight has stretched
a little further open.

Not that night will arrive
any later than yesterday,

but rather yesterday's light
today dares to linger
for a longer interval

of dispersed intensity,
with the bird's song registering
the pain of aspiration.

Spring is hatched here:
in all this sweet-strained vigilance

to be slow-born,
shoot by missed shooting,
song by belated measure,
ribbons in heightened response
alone co-incident—

whirling their contrived rainbow
around the dusky common.

VII

Until one morning
the path plunges into a dell
at the foot of an arched
iridescence.

And lemon-light
streams forth aslant
from the far hill through the rainshine,

to strike the serried rows
of bare trees a radiant emerald,
rendering each one
a vivid creature
of intelligent limbs
and rapt-poised endeavour.

From the robbed to the robed,
decked-out in free booty.........

.........but I cannot write this;
it far exceeds me.

Needing no alien embellishment,
its own dream of day—
without stealth but without warning—
has at last overtaken
the drear solidity
of night's removals.

ON THE DIAGONAL

The serried bank of snowdrops
wrenches the heart out of the day,
beneath the breaking bank of mist
in exchange of a sweet
unbearable prescience.

The long-held descant of unbroken white
does not rival the striated spangles
clustering crystalline
in their sloped shelter.

Nor will their imminent fading
serve the sky only,
nor yet the earth.

Their promise is for the vast between
of blue shadow positively applied
without negative echo of hills,
nor tribute paid
to their bare and unadorned protruberance.

Such eyes swim
in and out of the winter trees
deliberately placed
as isolated obstacles of unimpeachable dignity
for a visual bagatelle
across the fenland boardscape.

Always veering, never erring,
our zigzag gazes cannot fail to meet
at any distance.

They slide aslant each other
to be transmuted
into mutual touch.

Like posted stars
glinting beneath the veils of their misty envelopes
on their diagonal slide
into trusted obscurity

on the foggiest morning
of sure transport
by infallible pre-arrangement.

ON THE LIZARD

The sea binds the world
in weeping.

The sea hurls its sorrows
back at the lands
that have forgotten them.

It exceeds the boundaries
of oblivion
that the harbour erects.

And its storms of anguish
may yet still damage us
despite the red-black serpentine.

Yet the sea also heaves
with the higher currents
of celestial fusion
that it mirrors, movingly.

Its misery
and tremendous liquid gravity
always shimmers and varies
with the unison of redeemed bodies'
infinite dispersal.

THE SHIRE WOOD [4]

The county extends only
to the wood within it,
like a woman swathed
in her own shadow,

or a man lost
in the forest of his own loins,
condemned to hunt the pure umbrage
as it flits hither and thither,

in and out of his own trees
which grow fast in her chase
as the emplotments of freedom
outside the law

yet still within the monarch's sway,
who enters here as one unknown
yet welcome—couched in darkness
that drifts across the twin lakes of Newstead,

to learn the bell's tones and the tangled passages,
a bridled archway and a cowslip's covert.

Offences of game are here venial,
but the erasure of vert, forever mortal,

---

4. I.e., Sherwood Forest, the wood of Nottinghamshire.

for its history is justly littered
with the stained jerkins
of those who neither tilled
nor fought, nor contemplated.

A history pausing still to plead for nobility
bow-drawn from the nobly designated,

since no formal restraints
will ever adequately govern our ruling
and the ignoble foresters still shoot on sight,
at the stroke of a pen for lenient offences.

A county collapsed back
into its own forest. Hidden in its own caves
in order to escape its discoverable links
with the rest of the kingdom.

Withdrawn wholly into its own
reserve of imagination

where the wild things roam
and interweave and thrive
in a fording of freedom
under the dukes' nightfall,

over the scoriac surfaces
in neighbourly parallels
that forge furrows
raised within slumber.

Invitations of abeyant pathways:
the skulking avenues
open surely upon those sorts of adventure
which they alone may enliven and decorate.

A shire shrunk to its own wood
like a garden enclosing itself;
an aberrant set of one most general member,
the call to utterly protected wandering,

to re-trace wild ways
already nurtured,

pursuant of a fold within that outwardly defines it
as untraceable and elusive.
Our secret bed, alone with our own prey
in mutual rapture.

The chase as love, love of the chase here.
The exception as forever the essential:
the outlaws lone and loyal sway.
Vast purple clouds descended.

And the rainbow drawn,
all wrath now in suspense
for the duration of love's *fyndinge*
and its spectral dilations.

ODE TO SORROW

Want of all wanting,
that were the worst.

Mourning for mourning,
the direst dawn.

Unless Hell holds
an abyss of absence
in the heart of awareness
without consolation.

But no: that would remain
shadow of hope in order
that it be able to persist at all.

For this reason alone,
it would be also the work of love.

Still worse is the unshadowed,
the isolation of indifference.

So welcome need,
and welcome lack.

You alone may promise
and cannot forever miss,
if what you intimate
is bright truth in her
native radiance.

NORTH OF THE TRENT

Grains of gold are
dispersed through the firmament
in evening abundance
from the back of the lorry.

It is cooler now and time
for a harvesting of sunset.

Spiralling down towards the Trent,
but first teasingly up, over and round
a golden shoulder in mock *anabasis*

across the dark-blue watery enticement
of dumbles[5] scarcely visible
until they disclose themselves
as shockingly delightful rifts
in the level complacency of gazing;

through a labyrinth of hedges,
past ponds secreted like gardens
and dream-bestrewn meadows
in their most pasturing humility,

---

5. See, again, the footnote to 'Turnings' above.

I am walking in the sky over land
always about to vanish into vapour,
which offers the sad-sweet longing
of its open English horizons
that neither assert a finite barrier,
nor defer to a level infinite.

They are more painful than the falling bell-cadences
which will lure me eventually homewards,
and whose lesser hurt consoles me
through its more explicated resonance,
matching the benign mystery of horizon
with its still terrestrial otherness,
by a vertical mediation of
sad tumbling heavens,
elevating us through their headlong
yet measured evening downfall.

Both distances will wind around
my redbrick chimneystack
and penetrate my fireside gleanings.

PARTICIPATION IN THE PÉRIGORD

All that is past is gone
and we work for a future
that will at once be past also.
It is the transition, life-to-death
that is the real thing, holding
as not holding for the course of time.

But how can this be there,
except as the trace of passages
which space is generous enough to receive
as marks upon her body:
ravages, ecstasies or ornamentations.

These traces, these tombs, these monuments
do not simply record, but in recording
constitute our life as that which is
always already timed as over.
The immediacies of sorrow and rapture
like wraiths were forever fleeting
and now they are but scarcely remembered,
for all our guilt and anguish
at inevitable loss of fond recall.

In subtle yet stark contrast,
our childhood regions,
along with our ancestral stone mysteries
abide to be revisited uncannily ever-again
and yet always with a new echo
of the greater strangeness
of the very first time.

But as we get older
our still surviving acquaintances
acquire the same texture
as the ancient monuments.
The same crumbling surfaces,
which appear immune to death
far more certainly than
the soft, vulnerable skins of infants.

Illusorily so,
but then their final vanishing
startles us as if Stonehenge
were magically removed again
by Merlin from Gaul's northern island.

To visit them or to discover that they have arrived
by some mystical transport
from their rumoured still-being-there,
is to know that all your past being-with-them is as nothing
and that you must now begin again
at the very last, while there is still but yet scarcely time,
with a familiarity that is only so
because of its strange impenetrability.

And now the Nazis have forever departed from the Périgord,
together with the resisters
and the massacred inhabitants of whole villages.
It makes no difference to these places
that are once again now fully populated.

But the discoveries in the deep remain.
The subterranean cavalcade still thunders beneath us,
horse blended with bison; deer on deer.
The doe drinking forever in the gently abysmal crevice,
the legs and haunches of the horse
emerging from the rock into the psychic flatness of the graphic.
An underground womb-sea of resurging forms,
the quick work of the fleeting light,
the shade upon echo of respect for previous workmanship,

in coded interplay of blue and brown,
as the rocks' fixed swellings lend dynamism to bestial stillness,
the varied cinematic flickerings causing a dark body
to vacate a less-dark wall and so the ideal of species to emerge
obscurely through its imagined instances
that deflect deftly the real ones,
in subtle gradations of size, form and pigment,
and then the species to merge with species
right up to humanity, also universal
between its *eidos* and manifold exemplars.

The superimposed animated seasons
Of Spring horse, Summer auroch and Autumn roebuck
captured in their transiency,
along with the astonishingly angelical expressions
on the animal faces
and the uncanny presence of the unicorn,
as if fictional beasts were as ancient as the real ones,
and as generally fixed in their types and typologies.

Original gratuity, as old as us,
unevolved and unevolving,
in its hold upon the inexhaustibly eternal.
That which Vichy in its stratified racism
fraudulently declared to be forgery,
revealed anew by the Toulouse *abbés* in their dusty soutanes,
with their strutting local boys to assist them.

Later, the Parisian *savants* arrived to half-despise
their amateurish and ideological efforts.
But were they quite wrong to find here the Grail already?
The signs and tokens of our redeeming passion?
Despite dark sorcery the commencement of communion
of elevated and wounded spirit
with the created, material and animate?

For as one deer licks another, this charity
is rendered perpetual
by virtue of the hard mercy of the rock-face,
so that beneath the ground
we find not death
but that which life has left,
surpassing death itself.

Like the Archangel's sure hurling of the sword Durandel
back into the love-rock of Christendom
from Roland's plight at the dire pass of Ronscevalles.
And the black virgin also there in her hidden niche,
that cleft we must again enter
if we are to sustain the broad waters' flow
of France's humanely shallow and stately rivers.

Walking in the Périgord,
a hidden turfway once more inducts me into a new meadow,
past another nut-orchard,
holding the dark woods always at a distance,
always encircling.

COSMOS

Why is the day here?
And why is it now the night?

The earth has newly evaporated
into the distance of the sky.

Continuously,
the world preens herself.

Turning to face us
behind a screen of dark trees,

she is appropriately incidental:
our only one and all.

By means of more agile labour
we may yet entice and save her.

THREDDLETHORPE SANDS

The day here fills the scope of the eye.
A vast bulge of blue before us and behind.
But where we all sit, there is there forever darkness.
Ranged alongside each other all before
the one same passive intellect of the sight,
groping to grasp our fellow voyeurs
quite hopelessly.

Unless we meet together within the clear spectacle,
beheld *ensemble*, in the sky's inverted vessel.
Cherished there, as held in a vast stranded dome
that is crashed to the sandy floor, with no alien survivors,
suppressing forever every constructed pillar,
every artificial edifice.

Instead, the sands alone. The sands stretching
beyond time northwards and past the future southwards,
all the way from Spurn to Thames-mouth, a transfinite basis
for an infinite arched cerrulean and an infinite
stately imperceptible inrush,
scrolled here and there on a regular sandbank
of the Lincolnshire ocean.

Our vision, like a bow forever yet
undrawn. Thwarted further
by our standing on the ground
of a rival semi-spherical arena.
As if we could never quite grasp our height,
just as we can never quite stand
within our own envisaging.

Hobbled from the first by the earth our sole support,
never can we hope to see what lies beneath us.
Caving, we simply lower the floor-level
of our still same habitation.
To be human is to stand erect,
and to stand is to be upheld by the invisible.

Nor do we merely see within this half-bubble.
It is rather the very shape of vision itself.
The eye meets inevitably
with this matching immense but always half security,
terrifyingly sublime but semi-tranquil,
which is why all the Midlanders
visit this partial vastness as if it were their oldest home.

Nor can we even see
beneath the middle of the bow's string.
Never sink, like the light's pupil beneath
the horizon of its tidal iris. Rather, our feet have settled
on an unsinking sandy floor
precisely at the half-way point of our seemingly
possible envisaging.

Likewise we cannot receive all in
a single glance,
our entire standing within the dome of existence.
The best we can do is to lie down
in order that the two hemispheres
may after all coincide with and complete each other.

For then we renounce
the illusion that we may travel without
the fallen dome. Then we also know
that we lie on the very bottom of the world.
Then we can but wonder
not at what is to be seen outside the bubble of vision,
nor at what is to be delved
beneath the floor of the human firmament,

but rather at what surrounds and succeeds
that which may be envisaged
not by us merely, but envisaged in principle, at all.
And at what vertiginous depth
opens beneath any ground
that a body, however long-buried,
might conveniently lie upon.

ROGATIONTIDE IN ENGLAND

Isle of low mists, isle of high voices
vanishing evermore impossibly upwards;
isle of luminous shadows, isle of perpetual weeping,
isle of sighs and choked-back glimpses,
you soothe us with your muddied margins
and veiled horizons,
your merging elusive contours,
and rain-soaked intimacies.

You cast a veil of respect
over our inner anguish and confusion;
you permit the constantly-new parade of gentle pretence
and half-deluded dramatic fantasy
that suits those instincts which barely lurk
behind the raw unfinished British faces
more adapted to *faerie* and so
seemingly embarrassed and awkward
to be amongst their own humankind.

Why then, amidst the blown blossoms,
streaming-forth from nature's ready-made white bouquets,
in bridal springtime above a green canopy so bright
it can only have been luridly dreamt
as we couch all day beneath a lowering sky
whose grey sometimes transmutes
to a promising pearl of ethereal delicacy,

do certain of your grey sons
celebrate an exactitude of observation
that would never be possible
under your languishing, deliquescent sunlight?
Is it that they are afraid of the many presences
which truly preserve here the mystery of promise
as the promise of mystery even in the final
awakening and unveiling that will
once have taken place, soon after nightfall?

NUMBERED

Four shadows of three swirling trees
sweep the ground of the late summer
like vast fallen underskirts
whose crinoline-touch is
so perfect that it merges entirely
with the green skin of the earth.

Nor is there any interval
between me and the three serried gleams
that are your smiling lips,
your two complicit eyes
and the upswept brim of your varied hat
that shades us both from the one-trouble of sun-glare.

For your tripled gleam
is my quadrupled glancing.

THE PERFECT EVENING

The perfect evening
may cause one to wish to die
the next morning,
but not that very night,
since one desires to taste the relish
of the following dawn.

But after that,
a merciful release
might readily be welcomed.
After all, what could follow,
but an inevitable lapse,
a slackening of the taut, stretched
nerves well-tuned to perfection?
One would never be able to replace
their snapped, frayed or tarnished strings.
Even around some general future *acme*
the hosts of boredom would also foregather
as a result of mistrust, loss of rhythm,
fear, obscurity or doubting.

Yet what different delights
might one then lose from the store of the future?
This is why an evening is already for commemoration,
its passion to be not lost but otherwise repeated
in the commerce of daily festival.

DOWNLAND TWILIGHT

The Moon forms a disc implausible in nature.
Branches of different species combine in strange
but geometrical loops. Purple, unfurled from far horizons,
swathes round their trunks and precariously exposed roots.

The downs rise in sudden sinister gradations of marked lines.
Ever more new tiers and mysteries
of surreal outcrops, worked by lost hands
upon the countryside both with and against her.

Twilight claims slowly the daytime lives of cottages.
Their friendly red brick, their sheltering firs
that spread beyond their walls with perennial generosity—
all gathered-in by the night's unseasonal harvest.

Such a succession of faint horizons,
pleating, re-folded and then at last depleted
by the shadows' swooping descent
or sudden earthly arising. Who can tell which?

THE WINTER DYKE

The light almost meeting the waters,
the waters almost meeting the light
at the edge of the rainbow skirts
of early dusk. Every evening
they nearly come together
but the light sinks too far
beneath the level of the waters
to an unknown depth that is not the sea's,
and the waters are left stranded
in the night above them.

For no story is of the present,
every romance is historical,
unless to realise the moment
it exaggerates and already proposes to us
tomorrow's secrets.

But only in the manner of the wind
recalling old, cold heart-filled days,
with the frost stretching and the blood pounding,
while the mist's raw edge demanded
some rare interior displays.............

Now in the perpetual absence of their instance,
houses and trees and shadow
consort against the storms and raging winds.
They form gaunt huddled oases and yet
they are obscurely gigantic in their sparsity,

while the glory of the waters' high brimming-over
is the light still-reflected amongst them.

STILL MARCH MAIDEN

Still March maiden,
April's bride,
fair leaves fall,
then wintertide.

But the bluebells
are your eyes.
Blossom's pell-mell
sacrifice

is your lips' gain
in rosy swell.
They both remain
in frozen dell.

Still March maiden,
April's bride,
truth is hidden,
will abide.

Also in your night-time hair,
crowning snow for
virgin care.

Still March maiden,
Aprils's bride,
bloom wind-ridden
deep inside.

ODE TO FLANDERS

On the tower obligated.

Powerful winds instil tremors,
calling forth the carillon
to reciprocate and reinforce them.

I am rattled about
like a cog in the instrument of timing.

On the green hills of restored bliss,
Jerusalem is descended in discrete clumps
like a herbaceous border
of turrets and gables.

All sprung of gifts,
occupying diverse roles,
that are proud to gather and wary
within their achieved conjoining

salute the lamb
who has arrived whole
despite all his mercantile bleeding
from the Cotswold track
down through Thames' long coursing
and over the choppy waters
to the teeming lands
surveyed by the tall Belforts
to be turned into
the tapestry
that now displays him.

A higher loom of light
assists this miracle.
And a hidden pure ground casts back
the most intense shades
that apparently exceed
their pure white origin.

To be woven-in, planted, painted.
To watch oneself in many intricate
but placid waters, always rising.
To glide perpetually across
a land without friction.
To raise towers against gravity
upon leaky foundations.

This is humanity:
the descended real
consigned to a fusion
of pragmatism and dreaming.

EXILE

On the bridge of Babylon,
all are dancing………...

the white rocks and the blue sphere.
The white ramparts and
the further white rocks stark
with light at savage angles.

Primaeval motions in a round
when all are dancing…………
that were suddenly stopped
by an order of time without reason

to usher in the epoch
of the measuredly wilful

when he entered the cool tremendous
carved-out white palace
on the burning plain
with the whistling leaf-infused wind
curling around the dawn
to disturb all dreaming

and found a stark Islamic blue
and whiteness there to envelop
his lost pathos of purple,
far in exile from the gold-red sheltering
amongst the ancient olive groves
of the rich brown terraces.

Quite out of control, despite intention
of the fertile rolling spaces
of France so easy
and glorious to ride through.

From the heights of the courts of love
some are consigned to the dungeons,
and others elect for themselves the dangerous eyries.
The ladies stay still in their windy tableau
at their ease waiting
for a sufficient tribute that can
never be forthcoming here.

The heights presume downfall,
while the plains have long thirsted
for their due rain of blood.

Without his *cathedra*
the pontiff must now plead for
a glory of tribute
that is mere survival,

reigning in emergency out of a reserved
and absolute potency
that can only be exercised
by appeasement of dependency.

In a round, yes all are dancing,
the dance of Avignon,
the dance of death,

which offers all
to the volunteered source of dominion
and contributes nothing
to the human edifice,

since it worships its own strain
of pure self-squandering

and will not bend
to receive its own true flourishing
from an elsewhere
thereby celebrated.

SINTRA

Here was already beyond,
and they could only go further,
devoted to the murderous mother
who harboured their souls for
the price of steerage.

A contrived home far westwards
in its stranded sea-*galanterie*.
Here the serpentine stone-ropes bind
and exhibit what they can scarcely
be causing to stand upright for
genuine fecund habitation. It is all one illusion
of monastery, castle or surviving mosque,

enclosing a dark reserved courtyard of forbidden practices,
resumed in the sea-creatures' palaces
which encrust limpet-like the vast bereft moon-hill,
assuredly invisible by sunlight,
drowned by the wave that lost Atlantis and
later shaken by the tremors of dissolving reason.

As the Orient creeps round rearwards
to reveal the paradox and destiny of circling
in the scorpion balance of tranquillity and turbulence,
when to return is to set forth again
in wary exultation.

FENLAND INVENTORY

Interwoven with waters.
Towers floating on waterlogged fields.
Municipal emplotments.

Tossy today; her eyes are like curls now.

Picnic-boxes are sold alongside
spanners, big bouncing balls
and very solid tea-sets.

They would crack loudly.

LONDON BAROQUE

To let-in and exclude.
Permit and puzzle.

Make floors gulfs,
obscure light's sources

visibly over the gatehouse
that does not quite slide
into the railway-cutting
that it guards every nightfall,

nor ever really avoid this.
Nursery perils. Never solved half-enigmas
shadowing our bus-rides.

AWAKE

Men pass all night long through the Virginian woods
by no known footpaths, crazed
because they alone are of all creatures awake
and they long to sleep and to dream
the green-blue dreams of the trees
that go on and on and settle and manoeuvre
underground and shift there easily
or not so easily.

They know that they are noticed somehow,
by all of the inhuman.
An anomaly: the only aware ones and yet just for this reason
most cruelly exposed.
How embarrassing to be awake when all else
dreams unceasingly. How uncivil
and now indecent, against the usages of the woodlands.

The others stir uneasily
and come a little closer to the earth's surface,
at first just to notice its faint disorder
and the blind, lost, distraught creatures
who find themselves to be awkwardly upright,
hands at a loss, pacing the forest trails
while gazing forwards resolutely at the mere atmosphere
which intervenes briefly
between shrubland and starlight.

THE ENGLISH CADENCE

The sound self-complicates its fall.
It falls ceaselessly a fall forever newly resumed.
The intricacy of its falling redeems it.
The intricacy of the bell's lament
is made lonelier in the lonely evening
by virtue of the amber beauty
that in summer uncannily
displaces twilight.

And is like a trap to seal us
within the pathos of our most
unappeasable intimations
of prescience and mourning
for familiars and others
walking between them
in an absent solitude.

Further others elsewhere
may still carry my life with them.
That which I have said to them
awaits what they might yet still say to me
if I am to comprehend my own presentiments.
But I do not know what passes for them
in this present instance
and therefore my life is for the moment lost to me,
as suspended as when I first in childhood heard
the sounds of the English fractured cadences
falling into the night with a strange prevalence
of change through promise
that was already sorrow at a loss
that preceded even one's first fond ownership.

DELIVERANCE

Guilt is worse than unhappiness.
Grey squirrels part from the grey trees
like perfect fragments in sculpted motion.
I am the limit of the unlimited seas now,
stalled in my voyaging, albeit for glory.

THE FIERY MOUNTAIN

Strange paradox of Autumn:
we notice green now all the more
we are consumed within
the mountain's fire-spirals
that are rising arcades of burning beckoning,

and ranges and reaches
of banked-up hearths through
vengeful objectivity of private passion
in the wilderness homeland.

Gold-leaf markings strew the ways of the waters
while the blue background that envelopes us
shapelessly is at once most near
and extremely distant.

We have seen ideas, floating perfectly.
We have received them
within our bodies invisibly.

Now we are ready for what
shapes absently
the blue-smooth rocks
that are the colour of wisdom.

A VISIT TO WINTER

Caressing shafts of light pass through
the circumambient wound.
My binoculars discover
new worlds at a distance
that are not entirely there
if one walks up to them:
the purple-sheltered cottage,
which the white track semi-girdles;
the pearl-exploding treescape
that so gently ensnares the tumulus.

Riding this tomb, longways and upwards,
the hoofbeats pounding on the downland track,
I am about to pass over, once and for all,
during that delicious interval wherein I savour
the unattainable distance
which my binoculars reveal to me.
Terrible high-sounding tones escape the blue mist.
Nothing else does, but remains
in pools of emerald quietude.

Meanwhile I see clean across the house
through the front window and on past its
mirror at the rear, as if through and despite
a tree's complex branches or the massive fragments
of the ruined abbey. It is as though my soul
had threaded these gaping needles
and was another's, for all its poverty.

Out of the blue some towers emerge;
many twigs enhance them.
They are encased, each one, in shining ice
in order that a chill beauty may entomb
for breathless exhibition until doomsday
every unique variant of natural woodkind.
Even the shrivelled remaining berries, harsh and black:
they too are preserved here, in this precise idiom.

THE NIGHT-BEE

Everything opens to the round of black.

She is dark, dark with slippery darkness;
smooth and slippery for sliding touches.

The silky bodice becomes her
with a charm that is like a portal
of a door which doubles door
to allow meaning also to enter.

It has pointless black sparkly pointings.

The all-dark altered bumble-bee
zig-zags into that light
which she both misses and illumines.

With the concentration of all echoes
she hovers over my life as an angelic shadow
moving in mazy passages
across the summer fenland
in perusals of fervour, unexampled.

MOONGARM

It is amazing that nature
should be so prodigal as to
give us both blue-mauve
and pink-mauve in one sky
and at one season.

Nor is this all,
since at their intersection
something indefinable glints
that sends out downfalls
of the strangest silver.

It is all too densed by whiteness
amongst the woods for one
to be able to see the moon.
And yet her influence strikes
all around us in the now spreading

yet more alien silver
of an elusive screen through which I wander
as one so pierced by a spear within
that its piercing
seems to penetrate all around me.
Behind the screen I watch
the black trees growing straight up
out of the deepest pits
where lie the snaking streams
full suddenly of mercury.

From the sky's bruises
fall hard metallic raindrops
and I am reminded that in one of the pits
we have chained up Moongarm
the dog of truth,

sometimes feeding him snippets
just to keep him alive
but also angry until the day of his releasing
when he will swallow whole
all the tainted pastures.

This is in order
that we may then take up again
the scattered chess-men
from the precise places
where they were last forsaken.

THE HOUSES OF VIRGINIA

The common spaces are all hovels
where humans crouch, in a stifling darkness,
awed beyond meaning
by every dwelling of light
that is perched on a hill-top,
swept by a meadow,
shrouded with woodland.

Each and every one of them is a sign,
carefully crafted with porchwork and balustrade
like the letters of an unknown alphabet.

They keep the runs and creeks,
the rattling bridges
and the stone-gorged gulleys.

They are signs with doors:
unlike other signs
they possess an intensive interior
and point to nowhere
save inside themselves.

Not that anyone, hitherto,
has been deemed fit to enter
their souls of self-decipherment.

THE DREAM OF EMERALD

Outside our classroom window
there was an emerald field
divinely appointed for childish play.

At playtime though,
we were condemned
to a concrete stockade.

Last night in my dreams
I finally sought to enter
the bright-green pasture,

but an old-woman
even now questioned
my unlicensed business.

Foolishly, unbelievably,
I told her my name
under an incomprehensible oneiric compulsion.

Had I not done so,
then might I not have found
on returning thereafter to Gloucestershire,

to the old-stone house
with the golden nasturtiums
poised high above the far Severn,

that the meadow unplayed in
for pedagogic centuries
was now developed into an estate
built of mock-Cotswold stone
for long-distance commuters.

VIA MODERNA

The day vanishes
in its very dawning.

We might have soared through it
like birds rushing upon the waters.

But all was lost at the outset:
with crumbling nuggets of darkness
like charcoal we signed the warrants
of our own fatal autonomy.

They were derived from
the buried remains of the wood
that must haunt us long after
the final axe-blow will have fallen.

For in reality it is the absolute trees
that are but shadowed
by the gusts of 'little things'
of our own nominal sad contriving.

BEWARE OF THE SNAKES

There were many warnings of adders
at increasingly frequent intervals,
and he speculated
about the suspicious mounds of raised earth
amongst the wet tufted grasses.

Above, on the fir-ranked shoulders,
high cawing of rooks
closed the heavens from hearing.
Below, in the damp emerald basin,
the screeching of swans
rent their own dignity.

From the far-off outside
a woodpecker knocked eternally for entrance,
while the whipping-winding trill of the chaffinches
warbled the very vale into being.

Unassigned were the lucid jerks,
little twists of forlorn measure,
trebled mockeries in crystal,
articulated liquids, sobs and pauses
of a broken symphony.
Yet all these Marchtime voices
chimed out 'do not venture.'

Still though he was captivated
by the stream's silvery insinuation
of fast-shot unperturbed gliding
without notice through the lambent rushes
exactly on a level with its invisible banks
miraculously never overlapped
by sheer force of silent twisted motion.

As though its curves moved now
only through their own merged reflection
that made the mirror glide seamlessly:
surface through a surface—pure injection
of horizontal dance writhed out
through the lost pastures.

Meanwhile, the sun marched to its early zenith.
He tried to remember her face but could not do so.
Removing his coat with care
he bent covertly to the lone waters.
At the first swallow, he was taken.

SOUTH COTSWOLDS: EARLY SPRINGTIME

Tongues are fast shadows flickering
warm lights of the body intertwined
with their own echoes prematurely to speak
for the first time unruly under dense laws
that will far-flush a surface with long lattice-work
intricately aslant the high pastures where
no drownings may intervene to stay
the slow lure of cosmic reflection.

We are the hillsides chanting across themselves.
They are humanity already laid
to aeons of articulate rest.

BIOLOGY

Butterflies like celandines
adrift from their moorings.

There is a romance
between the flight of insects
and the rootedness of flowers.

That flowers so earthed may turn their heads
for seeking.
That insects so wandering may alight
with grace upon a stamen.

Celandines like butterflies
nestling as a flock of yellow.

So green the bank that is chosen.

ODE TO CELANDINES

Celandines are so much yellow strong butter
licked firmly such that it sticks out
in several radiant tongues silently.

As yellow they are divided
and circled in order to radiate 'Celandine'
in a thousand largely little
firm delicate crowns that reach much further
than monarchs' furtherings.

O yellow affirmed furthering yellow
on far banks clearly casting your surety
without attorney.

O celandines.

LOCAL APOCALYPSE

Twilight near Tarlton.
Light seems to belong to the land.
Darkness is coming down over the light
of the land like a dreadful vast wing.
With the vanishing of the day,
the lane will be gone also.
Then where will I be?

In the last seconds of the manifest,
I glance back again at the oak tree:
it's branches frazzle out in wild rigid zig-zags,
whose spontaneous growth is perennially
of the last instant.

Behind the high blend of hedge and tree-trunk,
sheep are glimpsed in their spectral pasturing.

They feed the last of the daylight,
only just visible.

THE EARTHLY PARADISE

'The Vicar is composing
metaphysical images in his study.
Flossie, Barnaby and Maud
are roaming the Somerset countryside,
their faces daubed with sticky jam.
His wife floats about the village
in dresses of diaphanous tulle.
The bees are buzzing
in and out of the windows
of the huge rambling vicarage.'

As he writes this he feels
enormously stilled within the dream:
anchored to its very vapour,
filmy essence and obscure drowned roots.
It is far more than mere consolation;
rather, what is happening to him now
seems but a faint blemish
upon the perfection of his abiding within a scene
that he does not so much imagine
as actually conjure.

Tomorrow he will not be any longer exactly here
and soon in another place altogether.
Already the present moments of his house
hardly seem to happen any longer.
He does not really attend them
and not simply because he fails to attend to them.

He cannot be there such as to leave any real trace
and therefore in any real measure.
He is only there for a duration
and therefore in no real abiding instant.

But in the Somerset vicarage,
there he is for always.
Forever moving in and out of a summer's day
like the bees entirely unperturbed, unmotivated
and unexampled.

THE DOOM OF MORTALS

The doom of mortals
is to love mortals,

to see as abiding,
what merely vanishes.

An appropriate love
would be for the eternal,

yet the invisible
leaves them empty,

so while some scions
of this reliable

still officiate in
cold stone cloisters,

mainly the desperate
pursue the fleeting,

fired all the more
as their fuel is consumed.

Neither make
for ready companions,

so mortals have resorted
to the pure intellects

or the fair, faint
overlapping presences.

After all, their doom
is here thwarted.

Traces of lightning
instead pursue them.

AROUND SIDMOUTH

Silver upon silver rising of nebular glory
that is fallen within the ozone for safe sure-keeping.

Eerily we expect a noonday moon more appropriate to guide us
than the missing sun dispensed with for starlight,

multiple and teasing, with an obscure grey humour
that concerns perhaps the uncertain border
between what shimmers still and is now already faded.

We walk suspended in the delicate kingdom
whose subjects are perennial guests:
unwanted, scarcely welcome, yet without fear of banishment.

Where gently warm peach-light nestles in the feathers
of the various greys, its weak yoke never quite hatched here
to create a certain mood or a distinctive movement.

Rather, our steps hover beneath this slight saffron effulgence,
uncertain what to celebrate or even to rejoice in.

Always within strangeness: at the edge of the familiar island
that might now be of ocean anywhere,

marking time over territory most certainly for a purpose,
yet for now a purely unknown one,

since all the cosmos seems to build up
to this mere conscious tracing
of its own strange lineaments of self-recording
without loss of any detail: triassic before Jurassic;
the minute sea-creatures now known as distinctive typefaces.

Meanwhile the peach is burned to umber at its sere edges,
the mist is descended upon the unwary walker,
the way back for tea is suddenly uncertain............

Then the miracle emerges of day beneath the shroud,
of light below fog streaming in with the tide
in a thousand star-sparkles from a time before the sun.

To that age in the late afternoon we seem to be returning,
as the mist confers upon us its benefit of immediacy
that we may serve time within an obscure entitlement.

After the desolate messages, the deceiving screens, the words
of infinite guile without grace of abjuration,
the way can be trodden again
with its secret detours through Saturnian camps
and red rocks flung seawards.

ONE GREEN DAY

One green day
rising
    with you above
the valley deep
        with promises
to market now
        the road
            so steep
a gradient of dreams
so light
    we rise
together and the vertiginous is wanted
for its near verticality
            which is you for me
eased just enough from the precipice
for us to glide upwards thrilled
by the terror
    and yet the ease
before the plunge sideways
            delighted
by the green sheltering deviation
that lies still higher yet before us
            you beside me.

The Legend of Death

Preface

THE VESSEL AND THE RING

The *Legend of Death* is a long poem concerned with the relation between myth, religion, and locality. More specifically, it concerns the identity of Britain and especially of England in relation to its double mythic legacy—Celtic and Scandinavian—and to the coming of Christianity.

Much has been written in recent years about "local theologies"—and often by people who wish to express only the most banal universalisms—but perhaps it is only fully possible to convey the link between story, creed, and place in a poetic idiom. This permits one to display the complex and converging crosscurrents that occupy a twilight zone between fact, rumour, and fiction, as well as between space, time, and eternity. It is here that the deepest and so most religious "identity" of a region is to be located.

The poetic mode also potentially allows one to do justice to the sheer multiplicity of any concrete identity, without thereby losing a sense of its distinctness, nor of its enigma of character, which is paradoxically proportionate to its definiteness. It is also perhaps within such specific enigma that the universal can be most indicated, because the true universal lies beyond abstraction as the original transcendent source of all things.

In the case of Britain, some of these general considerations are acutely exemplified. As an island it has stood from very early on at the crossroads of different cultures. If it possesses any identity, then this is a result of continued (and very much unfinished) cross-fertilization, and is in many ways, as Rudyard Kipling saw, more to do with location and persistent spirit of place than with ethnic tradition. And even in terms of location one is often talking about trans-location, a constant echo of "elsewhere," both real and imagined.

To emphasize this, I have deliberately approached the question of British and of English identity obliquely, by beginning the poem in the "other Britain," namely Brittany, on the mainland of Europe yet enjoying a semi-insular isolation. What the nineteenth-century Breton folklorist and radical republican Anatole le Braz termed that region's "legend of death" is also the primary mythic frame for the whole work.

Eventually, however, the poem moves from the English South West through what was once northern Wessex and Southern Mercia to East Anglia, and from Celtic to Scandinavian mythic invocations. The Celtic element is seen to be to do with origins, both eternal and temporal, and with a spatial, preternatural "elsewhere" that may be either sinister or redemptive. The Scandinavian element is seen to be to do with final ends and with a current historical finitude always surrounded by horror, yet mitigated by human warmth and artistic ingenuity. In either case, there is also a great concern with romantic love and betrayal. Here the Celtic tradition is more focused on the passage from human to divine love, the Scandinavian upon a final and miraculous "return" of human love upon this earth.

In both cases also, the mythic themes are focused about a single object. Prehistoric rock designs in the British Isles, as in the rest of Europe, show an obsession with the "cup and ring" symbol. Here I have focused respectively on the later Celtic interest in the cup or "vessel," and the Scandinavian interest in the ring (though that is present in Celtic sources also, some of which I allude to). The poem therefore sustains simultaneously Richard Wagner's double interest in both the grail cycle and the ring cycle in terms of their relation to Christianity—though it shares little of his metaphysical perspective.

Both vessel and ring hold circles: the one is the mouth of eternal and temporal origin; the other is the spatial gathering of unity, besides being the shape of human odysseys and of the entire cycle that pertains between eternity and time.

Both also are to do with gift. The vessel is the source of provision; the ring symbolizes the circulation of gifts and is itself the most exemplary gift as the sign of human bonding. But gifts are at once things and signs: they are supremely "intersigns," as Le Braz described the Breton symbols of death. As such, the mythic theme of the gift is appropriate to a poem that is about the intersection between material place and spiritual notion.

However, a gift may be a false gift. In terms of the Celtic vessel, there is always a question of unknown origins. From where does the gift arrive? From where, in particular, has your bride or bridegroom really sprung? Here one of the main, and I think "Celtic" themes of the poem, is the idea that arrival in either space or time mediates between finitude and the infinite. For the curious mark of the finite is that it is not, after all, a bounded totality. Instead, there is only ever "one finite" which gets ceaselessly interrupted by "other finites." This is why, it seems to me, the various Celtic cultures were right to see that the "preternatural" always mediates between the natural and the supernatural. There is something "more than human" about the arriving or other human reality "over there"—and beyond even this "over there," there may be other created beings not exactly human at all. Yet nothing guarantees that these "elsewheres" are also good, the sources of a nurturing and healing, rather than a wounding and destroying, donation.

In terms of the Scandinavian ring, this may also deceive. The recipient of the gift of a ring may falsely hand it over to someone else, or the bearer of the ring may not be after all the authentic owner. Here the sign-aspect of the gift betrays its thing-aspect. On the other hand, as Wendy Doniger has described, the thing-aspect of the gift allows one to counter-subvert the deceits exercised by its sign-aspect. Thus in many Indo-European tales (and particularly in the Tristram and Siegfried stories as here invoked) the original true owner of the ring is able physically to "catch up" with the signifying pretences and so to "usurp the usurper" or "pretend to be herself" (or himself) by once again wearing it. So because the ring-as-gift is a thing, it can be the sign of authentic identity; but because it is a sign it can also allow imposture; yet still, in a third moment, because the ring remains after all still a thing, it can undo this imposture and once again function as a true sign. Yet in this final, redeemed situation, the sign-aspect is not surpassed: the indication of this is the fact that, for a while, *only* the ring secretly identifies the true owner, because spectators—even bed-partners—imagine that they are still viewing the person who is (unbeknownst to them) an imposter.

This curious *topos* is echoed in the entire structure of the poem, in which ideas "abstractly" lift off in our imagination from places insofar as places are signs, and yet the poem counterbalances this by invoking actual journeys, taken today (and not just in the past) and indeed inviting the reader to "go beyond the poem" by taking these journeys for herself and so returning to the poem's original sources of inspiration. There is therefore much in the poem about the relationship between heroic adventure on the one hand, and writing on the other. Without some sort of record of heroism—however obscured—it is suggested, there is no heroism at all, since heroism, like the written record itself, must make some sort of honourable appearance in order to be, contrary to the sentiment of Gray's *Elegy*, whose "mute, inglorious Milton" lays itself wide-open to the ironic invocation of the earlier poet's "no cloistered virtue." Yet on the other hand, sign should not be taken as an immanent transcendence that leaves behind the in-itself-meaningless event, just as the hero seeking *mainly* renown renders his heroism ironically diminished. Rather, sign and narration urge towards a "gifted" unity of theme and activity; they should encourage us back towards a now-more-meaningful action and a now-more-saturated experience.

In this respect, while the poem clearly owes much to modernism, it is also implicitly (and at one point, explicitly) critical of it, insofar as modernism's proper concern for the "work as such" can too much pretend to leave behind the "occasions" for a work, which may be personal and intimate as well as public and historical. Accordingly, this poem does not at all strive for impersonality, though it tries to link subjective self-realization through expression to the continuing endeavour of self-realization of an entire specific culture. It is also hoped that it avoids some modernist obscurantism, insofar as most of the allusions are either self-explanatory or easily followed-up with the help of my endnotes and the Internet. (The latter resort now holds out an interesting new possibility of "exotericizing the esoteric.")

The vessel then, is to do with the ambiguous source, nurturing or poisoning; the ring is to do with ambiguous relationship, faithful or betraying. In many ways, it seems to me that the "dark side" of these *topoi* is more reflected by the Continental than by the British sources. Thus, in the poem, the legend of death is very sinister in its Breton version, but modulates into a "rumour of life" in its Cornish recension. We now see that death is not just the ultimate object of dark myths, such that life is purportedly exposed as death's legend, but also that death is itself merely a legend, merely the work of hidden, false, demonic poets. At the same time, the Christian "final sacrifice," which puts an end to sacrifice, is seen as a higher return of a "saturnian age" of star rather than sun cult, which was a time before the arrival of sacrificial practices in the age of agriculture and the domestication of animal prey.

In a similar fashion, the poem in its later sections recognizes an English affinity for the story of the loyal Weyland (itself a more benign version of the *Edda's* tale of "Volund"), which counterbalances that of the Scandinavian trickster, Loki.

So in the British versions of the two mythologies the source of the gift becomes more reliable and is removed from a sacrificial economy, while gift as bond also becomes, through a now absolute faith and trust, more secure.

This could indeed be seen as insular illusion and false consolation. At its worse, England (specifically) encourages a cozy blindness to our existential condition, just as the southern English landscape can seem soft and weakly beguiling. On the other hand, the more hopeful versions of the mythic sources can properly recall and yet redeem their sinister side, when one considers how the myths have been Christianized (and indeed they only descend to us at all in post-Christian versions). Here, of course, the Christianization-aspect applies also to Iceland, to Ireland, and to Brittany, yet in the case of Britain, the mitigation of darkness by the light of the gospel appears I think even more marked. To just this measure, there is more fusion here of the pre-Christian with the Christian, perhaps precisely because both things equally arrived in the island of Great Britain from elsewhere, both were initially alien and therefore both had to be domesticated together. And when one thinks more in terms of a Christianization of the pagan, then the landscape of the downlands or the fenlands is shown to be just as wild as it is consoling.

The various parts of the poem therefore compose a journey in time from the pagan to the Christian, mapped onto a journey in insular space from West to East. The journey is, indeed, twice undertaken, in accordance with the conversion first of the Celts, the lapse into paganism with the coming of the Angles, Saxons, and Jutes and then the subsequent reconversion of England.

Thus the poem begins in Brittany, to which exiles from the pagan Saxons fled, but from which many nobles returned to the old domain with the Normans, bearing with them much of the corpus of Arthurian myth and what became the literature of "courtly love." It then moves up through Cornwall, invoking both a shared culture with the Bretons and the unique Cornish myth about the journey of the Christ-child to this peninsula. The next two parts of the poem then fragmentarily retrace and re-invoke the birth of the European Romance cult from these far-western elements and then the merging of this cult with the cult of the eucharist in terms of the legends of the grail.

So far, then, the poem deals with origins and redemption and the cultural consequences of Christianity in the European Far West. With part 5, "The Advent Train Ride," it turns towards eschatology and so, also, to a non-identical repetition of the entire theme of figurative anticipation of the Incarnation and eventual conversion to its saving virtue. As this section is sited in the "middle" of England, it also invokes the coming of the pagan Anglo-Saxons from the East, besides the renewed coming of the oriental message of redemption. The poem thus travels back towards the Eastern source, which will also, with a circular return, be our final divine-human end.

Part 6, "The Song of Weyland," then recapitulates the theme of Christian romance of part 3. Yet in that part the focus was on uncertainty and betrayal blended with a hard-won fidelity, not necessarily rewarded in time. In section 4, "The Quest of the Vessel," this essentially Arthurian stress evolved into the question of the sublimation of love and the need to turn human woundedness into generous political governance rather than a systemized and socialized rancour. But the "Weyland" section is more simply about constancy in human love and the way an albeit beleaguered ingenuity can sustain this.

Part 7, "The Circulation of the Ring," which contains many direct citations of *The Edda* and *The Poetic Edda*, represents the "Scandinavian darkness" to balance the "Celtic darkness" of section 1. This is a darkness of fatality and ultimate doom, linked to the apparent final triumph of a bleak poetry as betraying sign which permits treacherous action, only qualified by an intimation that, within this stark landscape, the high god Woden may himself become a kenotic, suffering figure. In part 8, "In the Land of the East Angles" however, the smith Weyland's constancy which has allowed him to out-deceive deceit itself, now permits him simply to ignore the trickster Loki, and to sustain forever his own unity of art and love, sign and action, in relation to his "swan" beloved.

The final part is an epilogue that completes the tracing of an historical move from myth to religion to a metaphysical reflection upon religious practice. It thereby considers in a more deliberate mode the place of poetry, myth, and location in relation to Christian belief. The early Christian borrowing and adaptation of a "Platonic" idiom is here alluded to.

The last lines of this final section return once more to the very simple lyric mode that has already ended various of the "broken epic" sections earlier on. This is supposed to convey the importance of turning from a narrative to a liturgical idiom, and from the signifying invocation of the absent, to the renewed active inhabitation of inherited signs.

1. THE LEGEND OF DEATH

Other Britain.
Gleaming Leaves.

Fir trees surmount far
cottages nestled amongst rocks
like other rocks.

Long-leggèd ghosts
hide from each other
amongst the strewn stones
that may be menhirs
seeking baptism.

The last the last
victim
is always the current harbinger.

We hear the creak
of the trundling cart down silent lanes
at dead of night.
                      Just before twelve
the young fishermen are woken
by a tapping at the door
that calls them forth in a low voice
to ferry the dead over
to the walled island.

The last buried guards the cemetery.

Always there are two brides
in the two Britains.
It is the doom
of the Chateaubriands.

Isolde of either shore
verifies Tristram by his ring
which any may wear,
and yet which would allow him
to impose
also as the imposter

since it circles back upon itself
to close the circle of magic
and give rise to the questing subject
who can accompany every fatal exchange
to outplay its alien original.

Intersigns of death.
A white calm,
                    pallid torpor
bearing hairgrips,
                    a sullen pond,
a rocking cradle
to coffin the men of eagle-vision
unto the infinite
across the sea like a trembling mirror
with no image for reflection.

All this paleness of things
presents no nuance that could be named.
It is to blame.
          Blemished with absence,
the lure of the mordant.

Fruste. Fustian

that sails through a pale of vapour
far from the honey-tasting cider
served in pottery bowls with handles,

while a bouquet of rays
creates a temple vault,
light is piled upon light
unto the horizon
          as first separated
from *les ténèbres*.

This *leuer*[1] has been vague and strange
all day,
like that of a dream
for the men in the blanched boat

with its angel droppings;
horizontal like Cybele with the Christ child
or the grown entombed Jesus.

(Since we have killed God,
let us at least live for him.)

1. Shining, luring (obsolete French).

A circle closed upon enchantment.
And a quest arises.

No formula is required any longer,
but simply a question
that will unlock the spell.

Since without it the almost-isle
persists in its buried dreaming.

The doom of duality:
                      cup and ring,
                      cider and ale,
                      Celt and Angle,
Oxford and Cambridge.
The giant's soul is snatched away
and we never rest content with mortals.

At every wedding-feast
the phantom bridegroom arrives
to bear off beauty to his eastern sun-palace.

On every road
the faerie-bride ensnares the hero
in the spectral moonlight.

There is the dry cold before morning
and the damp warmth before evening.
Purple-pink of many flowers
in the in-between time.

A great sign, a lure.
Roseate dawn that is queenly.

Such gleaming leaves of chestnut
flank lanes without likelihood
down their routes to the sea.

And such diversely-coloured flowers are
arraigned along the base of the church-wall.

The *maquis* are still drinking at the café bar.

And there are two currents in the entire earth-ocean:
one pulled by the moon, the other by inertia.
At the solstices there is only weak water.
Strength awaits the Sun and Moon's
equinoctial concurrence.

Let me not be the last to die this year
and become the bearer of a curse or
metaphysical contagion.
Not even the pardons of fire over centuries
have cautioned this tale of division
and captivity by elsewhere

which is the moon-country for which we long
and where we half-are by presentiment.

The bruised clouds wounded
by the striking silver behind them.
The scallops and the hydrangeas—
blue mainly but also pink.
Voluptuous insinuating foxgloves,
melyn[2] gorse and ferns:
pure organic matter of Britain.
Flecked-fair these *feuilles*.
Fertile foliage, faerie.

But the death-goddess is guarding the long-chamber
loose-covered with cow-parsley,
                                    masses of buttercups,
corn-flowers, eye-bright,
red campion in profusion.

An avenue of large beeches
leads to her dire chateau.

Shores offer terrible ruins
of wars she has instigated.

Yet still we play at fairy *boules*
while longing for lost paradise,

2. Cornish for "yellow."

even though this too is now contaminated,
and the other denizens, those shadow-spouses,
seek counterwise to gain us.
       Hoping to marry
our mortality in order to escape
their doomed deathlessness.

Thus we are trapped with the shining ones
in a double *grimoire*:
mortals led to die through the fatal lure
of earthly permanence beyond the seas.
The others drawn to ironic absence
through the tale of finality.

Pursuing the wild woman on horseback
away from my predestined bride,
I am yet shadowed by a rival.
He has my crystal ring;
insignia of the archdruid
that will turn black at the approach of danger.

How can I be him wearing it myself?
How can I arise erect through the circle
to pose the question that is promised an answer
without privilege or concession?

Why does the singular man sleep still?
Why is it that I cannot ask why he is sleeping?

Instead Daimut still sleeps beside him
with her child for destruction.

To stay the torrent she was hurled
by her father Gradlon into the sea
for her waywardness
in welcoming the angel.

Half the time the bridegroom is departed.

There is the country of white corn: Vannes.
And the country of black corn: Cornouaille.

The fickle maiden
Is now the bride of Satan.

In a spectral light,
glimpsed rings of stones
and circlets of gravity.

In the close light that defines them.

Cerne,[3] *cerner*, discernment.
Ternir, turn, tarnish.

A white mist hovers
over one half of the bay
and yet the sea remains
emerald,
        turquoise,
                and opal beneath it.

Like the jewels and veil
Of a drowned lady.

---

3. Round.

2. THE RUMOUR OF LIFE

Belerion[4] where the Logos learns.

The Moon swimming silver-yellow in the blue night.
A dense and caressing blue.
Infinitely above the electric town
and the bay with the purple clouds hovering

till dawn when mist bears down upon fields,
shrouding gaunt cottages and long ranks of waves.

There's an edge to the land of making,
since raised beaches of lost summer-time survived
the glacial era.
                      Traces of visitants in the turquoise.
                      Moon of promise in the fuschia.
With cats everywhere like the Mediterranean.

While the seemingly alien towers of England
exert strange claims to pearls of spray,
granite striations, earlier mist-milk.

To broken casks of gold spilt out abundantly,
the whipping wind, cold-slanting sunshine,
spontaneous generation from dark pools
holding water as if in vessels ardently.

    4. Cornwall.

An ache is in us to behold their lonely calm
in the rift near the seashore.

Their construction of Cornwall:
                                  Lanyon's revolt
against visual space, abstraction, mere variance of viewing,
new games of duality and non-involvement—
a continental dire dreaming
to lure our peninsular tiredness.

While Iseult of Brittany pretends
the Cornish sail is black,
and Cernunnos draws Crowley to Zennor
with its orange water-flowers
and red-stained fuchsia.
With Lawrence he exults in the remembered burnings by the
hewn stones
and the more distant offerings amongst the pale-granite
masses.
Later Heath-Stubbs diagnoses unseen
a sloping of the land to hateful sunsets and a futile eschaton.

But this was to ignore the grace of mining
and of shaping always at work here.

Since what delves mediates,
as what flies bridges.
And what arrives seeks shelter
and exchanges.

Even the jutting land
basks for penetration
eventually.

Beyond humanity and its recent demise
other powers may seek us.
Sycamores, fuchsia, red-campion
and the wanton foxgloves.
Honeysuckle, dog-rose and oakum
deck *pons, men, lyn* and *gilly*.[5]
Adorn *bos, baly, gun* and *towan*.[6]
To *yeyn*[7] Zennor demerges the sea-girl,
gliding in crystal the sunk lanes
bordered by hedges fused of stone, grass and bramble,
blue-violet tansies, rusted-blood of sorrel.
In the congregation she goes unremarked:
a siren seduced by her land-counterpart,

pleading for half of her to be terrestrialised always
for him the bridegroom, figure of *ecclesia*
in this strange sea-version. So the one goddess seeks us,
her missing thing, in her wisdom of sea-brine.

---

5. Cornish for bridge, hill, lake and clearing.
6. Cornish for dwelling, farm, moor and dune.
7. Cornish for cold.

One visitation among so many.
Of boats to the sea, Gabriel to matter,
fishers to the sea and cars
to the wooded dells, tangles of black
and woven sleep, gold-seeping.
A mingled cacophony of gulls, larks,
blackbirds and thrushes. Ships supplying
paints for ships and paints for painting.
Pictures of sea-things; seas swept
to provide constantly solace for artists.
Everywhere perch the plump seagulls
so lamentably stranded. Replete as the air
and yet even so, intrudes the Paraclete
with his purple-tinged sweep of magpie-wings
clamouring for pearls, so infinitely rounded
and still discrete, loveable, devoted to her only
whose is the cottage-window upstairs,
right over the garden.

From bed to bed he leaps, eternal Tristram.
For now exiled from paradise
that was drowned in a night of terror,
as the Chronicle records and sunken stumps testify.
Leaving no footprints and yet his blood
stains the white sheets crimson. Like King Mark also
(or Lanyon gliding), who forgives his wife
her drugged flyting. No trace he leaves
upon the forest-floor
and yet the oak-branch betrays
his shadow there,
at one with the fallen.

To protect her face from sunburn
his glove covers a gap in the leaves.
Descended, hovering to shield her
from his own bright judgement.

Ad-silta—a.
She who is to be gazed at.
A T-shaped cross carved in relief;
so finite it lingers perpetually.

The sea is blown right into pubs
and not forever rules the cold goddess earth,
served by the one Sun,
calling for blood to fend scarcity,
worshipping limits, the same-old cycle.
Love of immediacy for lesser pain
still fades at twilight
when the moon lures the myriad stars,
their many lights bestowing a share
in invisible unity
not to be blazoned forth
or by any commanded.

Of another order: not the spriggans'
ghastly ruling of the moors' gigantic apparatus.
Ignorant of this are the dank *fogues*,[8]
where the woods covertly donate their garlands
on a summer night when the sea is turquoise,
silver-shimmer, golden-green and wine-purple.

---

8. Prehistoric souterrains.

When all the trees are assembled
(normally slanting, now upright).

With sea-thrift, sea-scabious,
hazel and honeysuckle twining in the distance,
arched over the graves of Iseult and Tristram.
Wild roses interlocked with stones in the hedgerows.
Curving borders of earthbanks, surmounted by brambles.

There is tiredness in the West, streaming
out of sunset at twilight.
A blissful fatigue of the body
releases the soul out to the waters.
Expiry in elixir of elderflower.
The psyche is co-original.

Once Joseph was in the trades.
When he landed at St Just,
God alighted with him for instruction.
With him as a child
to study all making, fairy-lore and the
arts of delving.
By three ways to deliver gold,
the price of all being.

They strewed flowers that took root.
Poor innocents came for the boy-child
that they might not finally diminish
but earn also the cosmic glory.

So strangely varied in colour,
yet withal combining
into a whole most harmonious.
Sown like gems which glittered with sunbeams
yet were in the round as mild as moonlight.

On Fiddler's Green the sailors are landed
to greet old comrades and their favourite fair ones.
The fay Queen's funeral is done at Lelant,
her people carrying poles of blossoming myrtle.
Solemn sermons have been recited
concerning the invisible world
that lies not above, but all around us.

3. THE BIRTH OF ROMANCE

Far is the land of the gift.
Lost to mischance once,
or folly of formulae.

The land that floated by ungovernable
art and prudence.
How was there once rose and flame here
before the door opened
upon a fear without warrant?

Not lost but well-hidden:
the site of the starred-tree and the token to plight,
that as a girdle may be undone
falsely borne, and yet re-knotted
encompasses again its true *persona*,
to bind two once more in the fallible skein of linear time
whose ends re-tied reveal the eternal more
than the unbroken circle.

For all the ascended tones of monks,
I could scarcely believe that heaven awaited
those who could not even retrieve
the lost paradise of earthly rejoicing.

Not to abstract and rise in French only,
but also to search out the specific trace
left planted adamant and unrepeatable,
I journeyed in English westwards,
seeking a clue to a mystery which
only the clue itself would first disclose to me.
Like a pure salve against the boredom of problems
and the worse despair of solutions.

Circassian sparkles. The fairy-band in her hair.
All aquamarine; such sea-eyes;
local art-shop magic.
The light elevations; heightened transfer;
easy currents through the crossed glances.
A book of recipes, of spells.
Follow the stages carefully and it will be simple.

But then the dark prescience already intrudes.
The labour rather breaks down in the end
to waiting and uncertain venture.
Can the promise nevertheless still linger?
A Saturday morning rustle;
some designs on pots by a river.
The art-girl scarcely there, iridescent.
Flashing like a slight silver fish
beneath the stream's runic ripple.

Westwards the hills circling the levels,
always re-arranging themselves in a dance
which you must master if you wish
to pass this way again.

From Somerset to Devon
the hills are closing in,
rising up to you within you.
But across the Tamar the close comforts flood away.
A new country is disclosed, stark and secret.
Wherever lies water.

At Plymouth I take ship for France.
But the lost land eludes me.
The wives of Brittany and Devon
learning of each other must now enter
after all the vertical litany.
I did not mean to shoot the doe
and cannot find the ship of Sheba
to bear me to the portended garden,
sheltered from the sea by a wall of green marble.
In any case the lady who might heal me
is taken up with another.
Yesterday, I received
the embroidery of the dead bird
but do not know who wove it
nor what song it silently records.
Back home, even my human vesture
has been locked in a closet
by my wife, long-pained by my absences.
Too late to explain that my presences rather
were the miracle of return to her my true-love.
From henceforwards I am as hunted as the doe,
though doomed to bestial vengeance
throughout the silenced future.

But still I have Iseult's love-token,
the ring of green jasper which enjoins me.
Over the ford to the Roseland
I bear her while disguised as that poor leper
which I am indeed, truly.
Bearing my taint she swears before Arthur
and the gathered relics from all the chapels of Cornwall
that she has had only Mark and the leper
between her thighs ever or always.

Truth bends to the word
which hides it.
For reconciliation with Mark and the *Logos*
Iseult wears a dress of Baghdad silk,
rare with white and grey furs shimmering,
and a gentle neck all-harnessed in gold,
bought by Ogrin the hermit
at the mount-mart of Michael.

To marry, to bury,
to market, to dance.

To Wotton, to Gloucester,
to Ciren', to France.

From fame and from bleeding
good fortune is leading

to birthright and venture
in spite of all chance.

By trysting, by lance.
By trysting, by lance.

4. THE QUEST OF THE VESSEL

But seek you first……………………
But simply ask………………………
At the Castle of Inquest……………..
After unparalleled adventures………

The gleaming woods
dark-rolling through the misty lands.
The high, dark rolling.

While the endless golds unfurl,
dark and sumptuously varying.
The beauty of darkness is here
and the darkness of the beautiful.

Hidden treescapes.
Involved ascents.

In Somerset is found
the secret centre of everything.

This land is anathematised.
As the swish of the sirens' silken garments
begins to becloud his intelligence.

He is searching for the secret which the land
offers and withholds endlessly.
The story of his searching will invent
the hidden object of the land that the land lacks.

Yet it cannot find it for him.
That he has never done;
not yet,
not on any day of this world.

He has not yet discovered the court
from which the land may be made bright again.

Throughout his misty and his rainy journey,
nature flowing with emotion,
its sorrow in torrents:
she is outwardly weeping; he is inwardly raining.
He is watering the black soil.
All nature's secret original growth
derives through his shed waters.

To weep and piss in sympathy with nature.
It is obscurely comforting: such an exposure
to the agreement of inside with outside.

Somewhere the warmth abides,
singing the nightway.
Is it in the flecked-fires of the trees?
In their new warm tinges along with
and despite the shudderings
and gustings of windlight.

The inner flames and the outer winds.
Everything burnished, buried and browned.

Mature radiance of passages.

And why does the grail appear
in so many places in Logres?

By gravel as red as burning fire,
over spectral waters far colder than ice
which turn bitter and green as the sea itself,

his joy at seeing the vessel
would be as that of the king of the fish,
exiled to land, returned amongst them.

The city of Sarras in the spiritual place.
Yet he already rules it, as in a nightmare,
and harries from that lost citadel
the castle of the black hermit.

Giving again our power to give:
the cup of earth, the first unravished maiden,
the voices of the wells unsealed,
travellers again to be watered
from the waiting wellheads.

His dream on the nightway:
Arthur the wounded king and quester
who has seen the Grail pass
through five changes that may not be reported.
No pure knight rescues the virgin,
but rather the secret ruler
stricken in the thigh by the angel
who traces in his blood the descent
of vengeance. By whose bearing
comes balm for others, and for self in mystery.

Radiant passages. Radiance burns through.
He searches the Isle of the Active Door.

Immense tunnels of trees; gradually more misted.
The woods darkening. More waters trembling.
Tunnels and torrents of trees.

Efflorescence of clouds.

Immense throngings, partings, gatherings
for sudden dances.

Round corners guarded by leaded windows
to the warm sanctuary of the hotel eventually
he is yet not equal.
Too chilled for it to cheer him.
Soon he must meet Argante in her empty cathedral.
It is too much to deal with for the moment.
All the rain, light, cold at twilight
amidst the dense tumbling woodlands
is still within him.
Suddenly, obscurely, this is the hour.

In the dark apses,
before the blue vast vitrail,
there is laid for foundation of Zion
a stone since the beginning of all things.
It is a secret fragment as old as nature,
of divine creation, yet of ours also.
The hidden primal invention,
lost to false seizure.

Without a celebrant there commences
the Mass of our Lady.
Argante advances.

Arthur is lost in shrouded mysteries.
He beholds women swathed in white silk
and before dark gates, a light is lifted.
Here begins the great fear.
Darkness of darkness, night in dense clusters.

Upon the perilous seat,
within the turning castle.

Can he give rule, and so rule truly?
Will he outdo the ringed table's
game of musical chairs
with always one seat
too few and one child forsaken?

Can he forebear to slay
the previous guardian and seize
the fairy-cup of meaning
yet again for always?

A new transmission passes.
Arthur asks. The golden bough is snapped.
A healing usurpation reigns.
And old men pass retiring ways
to peaceful deaths.

Arthur is married to the land.
The vessel hovers without arms to uphold it,
dispensing perfume and elective favours.

Silver and ruby shimmer.
Gloss of brown woodland.
The serried golds of Autumn.
Theatres of mist seeping.

They are plunged downwards
into quarries of order:
Bath, Wells, Bradford.
All the mists resume
their feeble strategies
for comprehension.

The landscape obsesses them
like the final bed they long for.
Never, never could they have done
with its risings and unfoldings.

Leaving Argante in the hotel corner,
Arthur does not even glimpse the Minster.
Soon she will proclaim beneath its inverted archway.
All the druids will be there, in the sombre torchlight.

5. THE ADVENT TRAIN-RIDE

Bells are of high music, the most psychic.
The past is pure clangour
and the future ephemeral.

The gift is of long hills,
old silence, childhood.

There is low mist with green silhouettes;
so objects defeat vagueness all the more clearly.

A weaving of the mist through black bare trees
which form a complicated loom.

The mist creates a cosmos.
Copses like planets. Vehicles like lone comets.
A white cosmos.
The roads high up
as if threading through the stars.
A sense of elevation;
of giants bearing one upwards.

There are hidden creatures amongst the trees. The landscape
belongs to them.
Light will appear again from the East
as always, this time an exception.

Low-lying band of mist with rising sun
shining right the way through it.
The frosted rainbow. The bright low stars.

Stone,
      ice,
           frost
                  abiding.

Human labour on stone.
The shaped world.
The psychic manifest
more in the inorganic.

A divine unity of art shown
more in stilled and lifeless water.
A single crystal glaze shimmering
over everything. A perfect unity of hill and sky
in diverse shades
of pale and purple.

This vast latent instrument
waiting to be plucked, breathed through,
struck for once rightly.

After the first arrival of the reed-blowers
the wind now rises from both trees and voices.
The black singing birds with their long necks
take-off to reconnoitre.

The train is a corridor of warmth
entering the ice landscape
which it reads as emplotment,
whereas the road knows it as labyrinth.
The sky is impenetrable white,
it is melting ivory.
The remembered surface of the dyke beckoning
is hardness
anachronistically moving.

It places the inn besides it.
The inn guards against the influx
of the far sea,
always here uncannily absent.

In the land of the East Angles
everything is bristling weaponry.

Their possibility of beauty is violence.

The promise of a piercing
that will heal
instantaneously.

But blinking awake again,
I realise we have just passed
Weyland's downland smithy,
his hidden red-gold ring-hoard
and the white horse
foaling her own clipped maintenance
down unlikely ages.

Something other, some lost power or beauty
is suggested.
But on the other side of battle-tumult.

Everything is opposed, yet strangely allied.
The secret recovered through its necessary traces.
All of the rent, the given
exposed as but a suspension of hostilities.

As forced as this and as ephemeral,
its stone like ice; its carved-out work like frost:
the church whose nave meets the transept
and establishes the tower
in its woven landscape.

Abruptly the cliffs of blue
appear above like angelic presences.
With rakings of deep promise
since it is not yet the night's blueness.

There is the milk of the dales
and the milk of the hillsides.
The hills compose themselves
for their own dance.
They drift away unduly.

They lie in a plateau
of undulations.

And we cannot be called away to where they are,
but from afar we can receive them.
By remaining on the train,
we allow their passing presence.
In the meantime the river
has decided to keep surprising the railway
which is there to celebrate its meanderings
and to elevate the downlands.

Since the upper air wailed for aeons
to be seen from aircraft
and the fields longed
to be fused in passing,

while back gardens groaned
through all the centuries
in secret longing
for dazed voyeurs
of their prized privacy.

Their boundaries intact though,
across the sacred distance.
So the railway was really the new work of angels.

West Angles: above, between, interwoven.
East Angles: wading the low levels.

Recalling the silence of childhood:
rarely phone-calls, traffic, screams, intrusions.
The past is given, secured forever.
It will need all of the future
in which to be understood.

While nothing more can quite count:
any more seems fractious,
mere repairs, doodlings,

whereas the past is a vanished and serious edifice.
We must hack through forest to reach her
like a sleeping princess
whose beloved features agonisingly fade from the memory.

Frosted masts above water.
Topmost turrets of deep-buried towers.
The tips of spires and twigs of branches
in a misty ocean.
Such seems the present.
Barges, cars and lorries
cast adrift from their lost moorings.
Suddenly floating pinnacles.
Trees adrift on the winter flood-tide.

All aspires for that future
which will be the real issue
of all our ascensions.
What is to come,
what is yet to vanish;
there is only over there remaining.

Behind of the Cotswolds,
ahead of the Chilterns,
on their own courses:
ditching, dawning, rising,
to leave us in our grades alone,
those barren sequences.
But bearing our glimpses, in the meantime.

With a hint of greenery in the woodlands.
It is the King's imminence.

A simple counter-carol,
and the rock of sovereignty is diminished.
Every person is now a subversion.

Caskets of churches in the twilight.
A high music—pure, impenetrable—
lies out in the winter's cold.

We resist it and wish to remain by the fireside.
Yet we know that our souls
without us desire it.

The flesh is baffled.
The cascading bells rebuke us.
We must leave our warm palaces
for the cold crystalline.

How have we forgotten them?
Who can it be, still ringing them?

How do customs always endure?
How do we throw off
                          from a level
to the highest?

How do we answer the downs'
unreachable riches
with our own
yet more piercing
and more lucid aspirations?

You would step,
I would step,
you would step again,

upon the hills,
athwart the sea;
avoidance of the plain.

Such hours to chance
of ours to dance,
wherever this may be,

your rills pool laughter,
Wisdom's daughter
(after thunder, lightning kept),
whose forceful hold is free.

6. THE SONG OF WEYLAND

Summer doings in the attic.
A dream landscape. Utterly unreal
and utterly heartbreaking.
Why does it pull at me so?
It seems unvisited, unrecorded.

At the same time, dry and tipsy.
Lonely in a peculiar, a quite special sort of way.
Lonely like sheep, or like their hidden lambs
unfolding. Lonely as if its valleys belonged
to a different and unvisited planet.
Lonely as if these places of Wiltshire,
although so central,
had always been somehow overlooked.
Lonely because neither grand mountains
nor sweet low pastures. Lonely because
neither lush, nor dusty. Lonely
like a threadbare carpet left out on a green lawn.
Lonely because neither lawn nor carpet
but both at the same time, impossibly.

Why did you first tread upon my downland,
bare-footed, with winged silver-slippers in your hands,
O ladies out of Wychwood southwards?
Sheathed in your white-silk gowns,
black gloves trailing, red-lips undiminished
after midnight, white feathers still so naturally sported.
Why did you stay so long only to vanish
before the very next evening?

Two are still pursued by others,
but the one who compels me, she I must wait for.

Lonely because the downs are the grey-green places of ghosts.
Lonely because they really desire to be always indoors.
Lonely because they are like something that belongs in a
nursery
suddenly transported to adulthood.
Lonely because they are a natural fortification.
Lonely because wrecked, lost and abandoned,
insistently waiting their time still to happen.
Lonely because poised between feigning and warfare.
Unlikely unploughed hills above the tilled lands.
Unlikely and unreal.

Now drift of my word-meadow tongue accompanies
the ceaseless smelting in my found smithy
under the old firs, beneath the crouched stones.
I count my clanging-fires of rings ceaselessly
and always there is one missing though they are all hers,
even the seven hundred duplicates.
It has been stolen and falsely given to another, the usurper.

Beneath the sun's doubt-disk I always ponder.
But I am long-since bound and dragged to the shore-line,
to the black sea of the south coast that is leaden, oily, stately,
clinging, insistent, remorseless.
Again the sun draws the ocean to the shore like a trawl of
                                              diamonds.
The sea is nearly night while the lands are a green
that is without all trace of emerald.

In their utter blanched pastel the downs hold sway:
so hard-edged and so fragile,
like the passing of a wave photographed.
Now the dipped sun has diminished the gold surf-flame.
The noble giver! Who has now betrayed me.

The downs' rise above the ploughed fields is so precarious.
They are frail like musical notations.
For what is this county of Dorset so scored?
The land continues like meanings of the sea.
Like a dream where waves will never break, but hang
suspended.

Its buried organisms rise imperceptibly to artifice.
Their deliberate shapes anticipate art,
while my human works settle back into the forms
of huge fossilized dragons, articulately sleeping.
The thinnest skin of green that I could find
covers chalk like a faded fabric, rent in many places.
I cannot decipher anything. I want to
and I do not want to at all. For I need to claim the land
but fear by doing so to lose it.
Since it is all mystery, and without *proprium*.

The sparkling shoal of diamonds arrived
with the incoming tide.
But the black tide bore my captors also.
Now I am held on a lost Atlantic island,
bound to alien forging for my new masters
who will send ashore my glistening wrist-clusters.
Will the frail hills support this weight of treasure?
They are so hard-edged and yet so soft in all their inwards.

The sinews of my knees are cut,
but I have forged my own winged footwear.
The prince of elves, of arctic origin,
I hover cunningly above Sidmouth,
before another geology.
I glimpse the sudden red cliffs,
the musical boxes on parade before the sea,
the chiming hostelries abandoning all restraint
at the last gasp of culture,
so agreeably tarted-up in the face of briny judgement.
As if boldly to assume that this alone might receive
a lone sea-god's triple acclamation.

So rightly to meet he who flies the storm easily.
I find the missing ring and mend it
amidst the gloss, the parades, the balustrades,
the terrifying brash red cliffs, their sudden breaks,
the confuting and the confounding gaiety.

Tunnels and tunnels of trees. Folding into you
and over you, you rich red lands.
Sudden gurgles of streams and still I seek her.
Only one ring left, but it was the missing one, the most vital.

Exotic surrounds of bleak wildness;
carved lone-standing tors.
I will now forge my new sword
Albion.

7. THE CIRCULATION OF THE RING

Screaming he took up the runes;
his eye was drowned in the well of seeing,
for his deeds are poetry
and his angels, the destined ones.

The runes you must find and the meaningful letter;
he himself carved some. They are made and stained
for victory. Also medicine and flyting.

Without a mark there is no wound or record;
no sea-steed to sail, to search out the gold
that is but bright wave-glance
lost to our hoarding,
yet hoarded in glory of the carved song,
adorning the mound-pyre.

Cold-mere washes many a day.
The black timbers under the generous prince.
Storm-twisted-elm-trouble
digs into man's encircler.

I go West over the depths
and I carry Woden's thought-strand-mere.
This is my way.

That I afar should seek
over the ancient water's awful mountains,
Elf-friend's island in the outer world.

A white calm. Pallid torpor.
Sailing through a pale of vapour.

Men are named by tree-names; ships; killings.
Blood benefits wolf: it breaks concealments.
Women are named by adornments, gold and jewels.
Our doom to seek them over the ships' slopes,
Through every snake-woe, under the world-hall,
while two swans still feed at weird's well,
the origin of all swans, lacking their sister.

Always caught in the one kenning.
Poetry is made of name and substitution,
but is itself named by the trope of the literal:
it is the mead of blood and honey blended.
Woden imbibed it, from the leaden vessel.
He paid the seeress with many rings,
trapping black-gleamings from the moving ground.
She repaid him with bought knowledge of stealing.

A warrior must know how to carve, ask and sacrifice,
but in measure always.
One gift calls for another.

The gold belongs to seas and rivers
and must return there.
But meanwhile its captured purchases
teach to Woden death's legend,
and he hears of the world tree's suffering.
Nibbled at the roots, annoyed in its branches.
And of his own bearing there, himself to himself,
sustained by sacrifice, that consumes the recipient.
This was the Asians' proud elevation
from Troy to Ragnarok, Surt's fire at the end.
He hears of the coming of the men of Muspell
from lands too hot, even to dream of winter.

'Help' is a spell against accusations
(but sometimes the ancients were all too coy).
Surt and Moongarm are coming. The Asians
have left Priam's hall of beauty and splendour.
Middle-Earth is deserted: they have sought misty glory.
Woden will perish: die the terrible death of the immortals.

Winter unites: outside is all one north.

There are three kings: High, Just-as High and Third.
The mighty gap was, but then no growth.

For a time Woden was replaced by a wizard named Oller.
While he sat on dark-of-moon plane,
before the hall on corpse-strand,
woven of serpents spines.
In the East sat an old woman in Ironwood.

He takes up the ring Draupnir,
stolen from the dark elves.
Ocean's fire washed with his eyelash-rain,
he regards its self-generation.

Eight further rings, but the one ring
first was stolen.
                    Loki captured it
near the black pool of Byron,
chancing upon it from the upper path
through the woods of evergreen.
Fen-fire: it is doom-laden.
Fated for further sad hoarding.

As poetry rebounds from trope to liquid,
Sigurd must later show himself for vengeance
through the ring's circulation at the hands of the death-
                                                -maiden.
Myself as another is the ring's seeming token.
Myself-to myself is the story's sure unravelling
when the ring is tracked in all its winding
by the subjective seeker.

Great Christ created the whole world and built
                                  Rome's hall.
Christ has his throne south at Weird's end.

Once Jordan's Prince did send four angels from the sky.

8. IN THE LAND OF THE EAST ANGLES

Weyland spies Loki through the evergreen woods.
He bears his own ring unbearing,
forged and not stolen,
made for love-bonding,
the true other in waiting.

And waters very secret:
distant ploughed fields
and nestling houses.

Dark above. Light below.
River edged by reeds in water.
Unsolid banks: the secret life of the river.
Beyond: the very dry black woods.
Another world crackling, creeping.
Light shining through.

The river poised between still and moving.
The faintest hint of drift.

Like an illusion, the more inexorable for its slowness,
for its being just out of the corner of one's eye:

the midstream source of a new emergence,
the co-running of linked streams, teasingly apart
and then again to mingle.
Deep old November source of summer glintings.
A raw black day and the uneven tramp to the black pool.

Blazing now to Weyland with surprise and recall,
a swan passes through the gold's trapped evening:
an only just moving hoard of blank memory.
Motes of light like insects; insects like electric fragments.
Blazing brown waters. Brown unbrowned.
Gateways of light intervening.

The moon slyly behind bruised clouds.
No land. No sea. No sky. No Aesir.
She is trailing refulgence.
Trailing white light in gusts, like denseless clouds.
The Moon sailing like a dream-barque to tease Weyland.
Her other world of another light;
her world of curtains, lanes and trysting.
By her other legislation much passes
while most asleep are covertly refusing
her drowsy call, more intense than the dawn's.

The black river. The black line above the eye.

The black line of river running past green lawns,
stone paths and a blue sky.
The river like molten lead, with an infusion of darkness.
The river perturbed, perturbing them.
The old waters sent down from heaven. The waters from the gods.
The river side-lining, over-lining their conversation:
Weyland and the found dark swan.
Meanwhile, outside the window, the river passes.
The flowing ditch of death, its black brightness.
Hope: through all the summer day
                                      this deep, deep flowing.

And the sky is rolling over the plains.
The fenland opens to them a new vision.
No folding layers of nature's hills.
Instead they stand starkly exposed on the minuscule surface
with gestures of verticality defiant.
Advent of meaning: houses, churches, a startling alphabet.

The plain like a vast hearth.
The sky like the smoking remains of an exhausted sacrifice.
This land of only the earth and the aftermath of cultus.

Grey spiralling, whorled sky,
swirled with flaming light.
The light flames over the green translucent earth.

Climbing much later up Sutton Bank
beyond the Humber,
up in the golden light of Autumn, ever northwards,
they survey the final richness of strewn leaves.
All the gold distilled into divine organisation.

Here the game of the gods is resumed once more.
They are vanished forever with the Queen of the fairies.

9. THE BUTTERFLIES AT DYKE'S END

Butterflies are like launched petals;
they are ungrounded flowers.
Gravity defying: their souls are in this lift.
Still they hover about blossoms
like Eros above Psyche.
They caress what they have just detached themselves from
sympathetically, like Bodhisattvas.
Soon they might take-off and leave for other planets:
more exotic worlds with palaces for butterflies designed
by architectural lepidopterists.

Their every wing is different
and without reason. They are not at all adapted,
but merely flutter about the dyke.
They still guard East Anglia from the Danish Midlands;
they are the permanently stationed troops.

The dyke stops at the fens.
Southwards it is like an abandoned railway-cutting.
It is now a route and now the abandoned railway is no faster.
Both ancient cuttings intersect
in a knot and tussle of paths for walkers.

Occasional gaps in the hedge alleyways
reveal a good view of churches and windmills.
Swaffham's double towers glimpsed through raised bindweed,
convolvulus, red poppies, ragged robin and cornflowers.
Phases of dark glossy evergreen.
The embowered path on the top of the abandoned defences.

Once ideas were heavenly and like stones,
trees or grasses. They were the patterns on the butterflies'
                                                                  wings.
The patterns of them all, more vivid than all of them;
they opened wings as if they were the gigantic doors of a
                                                                  palace.
They engendered flying palaces. There were ideas
and then their summer shadows.
And they opened to us like doorways;
ideas passed flittingly through the shadows towards us
and we dimly reawakened their pre-ancient lights.

Ideas never got stuck in our heads.
Ideas were psychic butterflies vanishing into cerebral thickets,
so dark-glossy, like the dyke's angular entrances.

Everything passed.

People formed the earth, raised edifices
and received inspiration.
They long thought through things.
Their wisdom began in cunning and rose to beauty.
They were not detained
by the immanent grids of abstracted learning.
All of the outdoors was a book to be traversed
With skill, endurance and attention.

For there is no truth in indoors labour.
Now other powers watch for us;
we toil for God no longer.

I saw you in the shadows,
I heard you down the lane,
I glimpsed you in the meadows,
I found you in the rain.

You soared above the bell-tower,
you shrank within the grass,
you guarded every flower,
you showed the way to pass.

You showered me with tree-tops,
you launched me on the flood.
You bound my gaze in silken knots,
you loosen all my blood.

Notes on Places and Sources

1. "The Vessel and the Ring" is set in Brittany. I derived themes and sometimes phrases from Anatole Le Braz, *La Légende de la Mort* (Marseilles: Editions Jeanne Lafitte/Co-op Breizh, 1994); Lewis Spence, *Legends and Romances of Brittany* (New York: Dover, 1997); Christian-J. Guyonvar'ch and Françoise le Roux, *Les Druides* (Rennes: Éditions Ouest-France, 1986) and *La Légende de la ville d'Is* (Rennes: Éditions Ouest-France, 2000); Jean Renaud, *Les Vikings et les Celtes* (Rennes: Éditions Ouest-France, 1992); Wendy Doniger, *The Woman Who Pretended To Be Who She Was: Myths of Self-Imitation* (Oxford: OUP, 2005) and Pierre Loti's novel *Pêcheur d'Islande* (Paris: Éditions Christian Pirot, 1993).

2. "The Rumour of Life" is set in Cornwall. Themes and stories have been taken from local folk-lore, from John North, *Stonehenge: Neolithic Man and the Cosmos* (London: Harper and Collins, 1997) and from Béroul, *The Romance of Tristan; the Tale of Tristan's Madness*, trans. Alan S. Fedrick (London: Penguin, 2000).

3. "The Birth of Romance" is set in The West Country of England (Cornwall, Devon, Somerset, Dorset, Wiltshire and marginally Gloucestershire). Themes have been taken from Lewis Spence (see 1 above) and Béroul (see 2 above). In addition allusions are made to J. R. R. Tolkien, *Sauron Defeated: Volume 9 of the History of Middle Earth*, edited by Christopher Tolkien (London: Harper and Collins, 2002).

4. 'The Quest of the Vessel' is set in Somerset. I derived themes and phrases from the various texts collected in John Mathews, *Sources of the Grail* (Edinburgh: Floris Books, 1996) and from Layamon, *Brut*, 2 Vols., eds G. L. Brook and R. F. Leslie (London: Early English Tests Society, 1963/1978).

5. "The Advent Train Ride" is set in Oxfordshire and Berkshire.

6. "The Song of Weyland" is set in Oxfordshire, Berkshire, Wiltshire, Dorset, and Devon, being especially focused on the Prehistoric burial chamber "Weyland's Smithy" on the Berkshire Downs. I derived themes and phrases from "The Lay of Volund" in *The Poetic Edda*, trans. Carolyne Larrington (Oxford: OUP 1999) 102–9, as well as ideas from local folklore. See also Tolkien (3, above).

7. "The Circulation of the Ring" is set in East Anglia. I derived themes and phrases from Snorri Sturlson, *Edda*, trans. Anthony Faulkes (London: Everyman, 1998); *The Poetic Edda*; *The Saga of the Volsungs*, trans. Jesse L. Byock (London: Penguin, 1999). Also from Doniger (see 1, above) and Tolkien (see 3, above).

8. "In the Land of the East Angles" is set in Cambridge and—just at the end—the North Riding of Yorkshire. It continues to use the sources cited for Part 7.

9. "The Butterflies at Dyke's End" is set in Cambridgeshire on "The Devil's Dyke," a defensive earthwork begun in the Iron Age and then re-fortified in the Bronze Age and the Anglo-Saxon period.

www.ingramcontent.com/pod-product-compliance
Lightning Source LLC
Chambersburg PA
CBHW020849160426
43192CB00007B/842